In a world full of hurry and hurt, sorrow and shame, loneliness and indifference, *Be Still and Know* speaks into God's rhythm of presence, peace, protection, and provision throughout life's storms. Deb powerfully, intentionally, and prayerfully crafts a study that unpacks Jesus' encounters with various women right in the middle of their storms. From friendly formatting to thought-provoking questions, Deb's words seem to speak themselves right off the page and into the room with you.

> Sarah Schultz, sixth-grade homeroom teacher, St. John's Lutheran Church and School
> West Bend, WI

I deeply appreciate Bible studies that invite me to explore the depth of Scripture's truths in ways I had not previously considered. In *Be Still and Know*, Deb Burma offers us the tools and direction to do just that. Deb manages to put a multitude of scriptural voices, prayers, personal stories, and reflections of other Scripture readers into conversation with one another. Through the journaling activities and reflective discussion questions, she invites us to join the lively conversation. And when we do, we will all be the richer for the experience.

> Rev. Dr. Timothy Saleska, professor of exegetical theology and dean of ministerial formation
> Concordia Seminary, St. Louis

Be Still and Know is a timely and enduring biblical study. This resource reads like an intimate conversation, yet it encourages faith-stimulating discussions within a group setting. Deb Burma's prompts to read and reflect provide incentive to slow down and linger in God's Word, especially as it applies to life's storms. This study also offers a rich opportunity for journaling, focused prayer, and personal faith growth. In these "anxious times" we are deeply blessed to find encouragement for our "soul amnesia" with stories of hope.

> Pat Maier and Connie Denninger, founders of Visual Faith™ Ministry

Reading *Be Still and Know* is like sharing a cup of coffee with Deb Burma and digging into Scripture together. We, as readers, are encouraged to be still before the Lord and rely on Him to be our refuge in the storm—a perfect message for these challenging times. Deb includes personal experiences and biblical insights, as well as many prompts to reflect and respond to God's Word. I am eager to share this study with my LWML Bible study group.

> Debbie Yocky, LWML Rocky Mountain District President and women's Bible study leader

Life can give you many storms—storms that may affect your mental, physical, or even spiritual health. Deb Burma takes your trembling hand and leads you to the only refuge that can sustain you in any storm: Christ. Deb is like a long-time friend chatting with you over coffee as you navigate the turbulent waters. Together, Deb takes you through eight weeks of diving into biblical stories, uncovering the lies the devil tries to tell you and replacing them with the truth and assurance that Christ proclaims. This is a study that I'll be pulling off the shelf again and again.

Faith Doerr, author of the blog *Imperfectly Perfect Living* and first-grade teacher at Concordia Academy in Omaha, NE

If you liked Deb Burma's *Joy: A Study of Philippians*, you will love *Be Still and Know*. Her grace-filled approach to Psalm 46 will help you engage in biblical and real-life examples of walking with your Savior through life's storms. You will study Psalm 46 in a compelling, convicting, and Christ-centered way in the quiet places of your heart. You will find comforting words of hope throughout this study. It's a must-read!

Kathy Pingel, director of women's and family ministry, St. Paul's Lutheran Church and School, Janesville, WI

When Deb Burma tells her story, you find that she is also telling your story. Besides taking us into her life, Deb tells the biblical stories of women caught in the worst storms of life but rescued by the strong hand of Jesus. Deb uses a wealth of Bible passages to give depth to each story. The women of the Bible have the same worries that we face, but Deb reminds us beautifully to find hope in the promise of God's R.E.S.T.: Refuge in His Ever-present Strength in Trouble.

Rev. Dr. Daniel Paavola, professor of theology, Concordia University Wisconsin

In the midst of uncertainly and change, *Be Still and Know* is both timely and exactly what we women need as we live out God's plan for our lives. Deb Burma uses the Bible stories of women who encountered Jesus face-to-face to help us see that our faith and hope are not based on life circumstances but on knowing Jesus personally. Be still, and know that Jesus provides refuge, restoration, and encouragement to all.

Brooke Hollatz, women's ministry volunteer at St. John's Lutheran Church, Orange, CA

Once more, this author has skillfully blended her experience and insight into a well-written Bible study. *Be Still and Know* is arranged in sections that allow for either daily study or weekly group sections. The time you spend with this book will give you daily comfort as you learn from Jesus, our refuge in the storm. It is my pleasure to recommend this Bible study. You will enjoy it!

Virginia Von Seggern, past president, LWML—Lutheran Women in Mission

Be Still & Know

A STUDY OF REST AND REFUGE

DEB BURMA

CONCORDIA PUBLISHING HOUSE • SAINT LOUIS

Published by Concordia Publishing House

3558 S. Jefferson Ave., St. Louis, MO 63118-3968

1-800-325-3040 • cph.org

Manufactured in the United States of America

1 2 3 4 5 6 7 8 9 10   30 29 28 27 26 25 24 23 22 21

To George and Elizabeth:

Nearly twenty-five years ago, you introduced me to Psalm 46:10
as you explained the inspiration behind an original work of art.
Ever since, you've shown my family and me what it looks like to be still,
to trust in the Lord through every adventure and every storm,
to know that He is God.

Thank you, dear friends!

Contents

INTRODUCTION

God is our refuge and strength, a very present help in trouble. Therefore we will not fear though the earth gives way, though the mountains be moved into the heart of the sea, though its waters roar and foam, though the mountains tremble at its swelling. … "Be still, and know that I am God. I will be exalted among the nations, I will be exalted in the earth!"

Psalm 46:1–3, 10

On a recent walk, I was reminded how quickly storms can come, seemingly from nowhere. This one hadn't appeared on the radar (I'd checked my weather app before leaving the house) and it formed without warning. The wind increased, and I was pelted by driving rain. Gasping for breath, walking headlong into the wind, I prayed for protection and set my mind on the image of my home, a reminder of the refuge— the shelter from the storm—it would provide.

I couldn't help but think about how often storms of life imitate storms of nature. Sometimes they brew slowly, and we are warned that they're coming because they're on our radar. At other times, they appear quickly, out of nowhere, and take us by surprise. Caught in them, we're pelted and tossed about. Their ferocity takes our breath away as we move headlong through the worst of these storms.

When have you been buffeted by the storms of life? Maybe you were caught in storms of *shame* from your past, *sickness* that took you by surprise, or *sadness* that just won't go away. Maybe you've been showered with stormy *situations* or drenched in a downpour of disappointment or *sorrow*. Maybe your whirlwind of *scurry* has brewed storms of your own making. Where will you find protection and shelter? What image rests in your mind, a reminder of the only real Refuge who finds *you* in every storm?

When our Lord says, "Be still, and know that I am God" (Psalm 46:10), what does He mean? To what or whom is He speaking? If He is speaking to you and me, how can we be still in the midst of any of these storms? What can we know? Where can we seek shelter?

God's Word promises that in whatever kind of storm we find ourselves, Jesus always comes to us. Where does He give us shelter and refuge? In our redemption, for He rescues and renews us; in our relationship with Him, who provides relief amid our storms or release from them as we rest in His presence.

In *Be Still and Know*, we will unpack promises found in Psalm 46 and fulfilled in Christ. In the first session, we will study the psalm in detail and examine a smattering of stormy situations. Then, in the following seven sessions, we will study a narrative from the Gospels, following Jesus as He meets various women in the middle of their storms and as He provides refuge, strength, help, and hope. We'll view those encounters through the eyes of each woman. Then, we will look at the biblical and cultural contexts to grasp better the depth of Christ's care, purpose, and attention to every need.

Most of the women we will read about here met Jesus with a cry, a request, or a touch, concerning a physical or circumstantial need. Maybe you've cried to Him too. Jesus responds to you as He did to these women in Scripture: with care that goes beyond the immediate or recognized need. All were changed forever by their encounters with Jesus. As their Refuge, He transformed their lives by His redemption, and He began by meeting them where He meets you: in the storm.

We'll explore how each woman's story—her storm—may resonate with yours. He sees every circumstance, and He hears every cry for help, for what you think you need. But He doesn't leave you there. He leads you in truth; He helps you grow in your faith, enabling you to see and receive all that you truly need. He knows your storm. He knows your need. He is your Refuge.

Life's storms take many forms. Sadly, we will find ourselves caught up in every one of the types of storms described in these pages. I pray that they may pass without blowing hard against you. But in this sin-ridden world, we will have storms, trials, and tribulations. Jesus said we would (John 16:33). In the midst of today's storms, may God reveal His refuge for us in Christ, the One who has overcome the world.

HOW TO USE THIS STUDY

The eight weeks of this Bible study are each divided into five study sections, forty sections total. I pray this format encourages you toward daily study and devotion time. *Be Still and Know* is flexible, so it can be used for personal study or with a group. Plan for twenty to thirty minutes to complete each daily section. You may, instead, save your study time for one or two longer sittings each week. Or you may realize that quiet time is hard to find, and you'll steal a few minutes to read and study here and there throughout each day or week. Ask yourself how and where you will be still before the Lord to receive rest and refreshment from Him. Give yourself grace, and enjoy these studies in a way that works for you.

Sessions 2 through 8 begin with a dramatic narrative from the Gospels. Deepen your study by reviewing the corresponding Gospel passage each day. In each session, you'll find two types of questions: R&R (Rest and Reflect) for personal reflection, and discussion questions in response to the study (answers begin on page 218; I highly recommend that you access them). As you study, highlight what stands out to you in each daily reading. What really speaks to you? You can bring that to the table for group study.

To wrap up each week's study, you may view the weekly video segment, where I join you to further unpack Scripture and its application for our lives. Turn to the Viewer Guide at the end of each weekly session in this book to follow along and fill in the blanks. Engage in guided group discussion with the question prompts that follow.

There is no one way or right way to complete *Be Still and Know.* May God's guidance lead you to it and His grace carry you through it. Trust the Holy Spirit's work through the Word and in your life today, enabling you to "be still, and know that [He is] God" (Psalm 46:10).

> I do not cease to give thanks for you, remembering you in my prayers, that the God of our Lord Jesus Christ, the Father of glory, may give you the Spirit of wisdom and of revelation in the knowledge of Him. (Ephesians 1:16–17)

Be still and know,

Deb Burma, author

A STARTER PRAYER FOR EACH DAY'S STUDY

God of all comfort,

Quiet me in Your presence today. Reveal Your refuge for me in the storms that I face. Teach me to be still and trust Your will; help me to know that You alone are God. May You be exalted in my life, Lord Jesus Christ!

In Your name, I pray. Amen.

AN ACROSTIC MEMORY TOOL FOR EACH DAY'S STUDY

Find your R.E.S.T. in Him as you remember who He is in your storm: "God is [your] *refuge* and *strength*, an *ever-present* help in *trouble*" (Psalm 46:1 NIV, emphasis added).

Refuge: He is your protector, your fortress (Psalm 46:7, 11).

Ever-Present: He is with you (verses 7, 11) always—even now, in the present.

Strength: He is your power source; He gives you His power, by the Holy Spirit.

Trouble: He is your help in trouble and tribulation—any kind of storm.

STORMY SITUATIONS

BE STILL AND KNOW—PSALM 46:1–11

My sister in Christ, I am so glad you have joined me. Let's take a deep breath together, find a place to sit, and be still before the Lord. To get the most from this opening, look at the preceding pages and read or review the Introduction. (Maybe you have already read it, but I know how eager I am to begin a new Bible study, so I often jump right in!) I don't want you to miss valuable details before you begin, so thank you.

DAY 1: SO MANY STORMS

DESCRIBING OUR STORMS

> **R&R:** What is the worst weather storm you've been caught in? Where did you find refuge?

The sky was dark and light rain was falling when I stepped into my SUV. I was starting my daily drive, just off the Dallas tollway, to pick up my husband from work. The light rain gave way to a shower, then to a torrential downpour. Changes came so swiftly that they caught me unawares. Halfway to my husband's office, I was driving in strong winds and pounding rain that created near blinding conditions. I didn't know what to do. I knew it was dangerous to drive through rising water, but I couldn't go back because the weather was worse behind me. I kept creeping forward. Some drivers sought shelter under an overpass, but there wasn't room for my SUV. Imagine my white knuckles, racing heart, and repeated prayers; it was my personal "Jesus, take the wheel" moment. (Thankfully, I didn't stop, or I might have been carried away. We learned later that the water swept through our friend's car. Praise God, he escaped from it first.)

Finally, my vehicle climbed to higher ground, and I drove out from under the thunderheads. When I arrived at my husband's office, I was so happy to see him that I cried tears of relief. I whispered words of praise: God had seen me through this storm.

Life can feel like raging winds and rising waters—a series of storms. We can't outrun them, and sometimes they catch us unawares or unprepared. Where do we seek refuge?

Maybe you have been showered with setbacks or harsh news. Perhaps you have faced a downpour of disappointments or difficult circumstances. Strong winds may have damaged a relationship. Maybe whiteouts have blocked your thoughts, causing confusion. Perhaps a storm of hurricane force has come in the form of a challenging child or poor health. Maybe you've been rejected, humiliated, or heartbroken. I could go on. Suffice to say, everyone's stormy situations are unique to them, and while not all of these scenarios describe your situations, they will not be unfamiliar. In any case, I want you to know, sister, that this book is for you, whatever your storm.

R&R: How would you rate the storms of life that you face today? Circle the number that best describes your present situation in weather-storm terms:

1. Not at all—the sun shines brightly

2. A gentle shower

3. A heavy downpour

4. A thunderstorm with strong winds

5. A hurricane with great force

R&R: Describe a stormy situation you have faced in the past. How would you rate it on the scale above? Where did you seek shelter or refuge in this storm? Why did you choose that refuge? Was it strong and secure?

So often, sunny skies fill our forecast, and it's smooth sailing. Ah, but then a squall emerges out of nowhere, or ominous clouds form on the horizon. Lightning strikes and thunder booms. We batten down the hatches, but that's not enough! Will we veer off course? Could we capsize? Drenched in a torrential downpour, we feel certain we'll sink.

A SHARED STORM

Maybe right now, yours has been a personal storm that only you or few others know you've been battling. While I can't know the stormy situations you have endured, I marvel as I write this that we have shared globally in a recent one. Millions faced the COVID-19 pandemic separately, but together.

When this storm cropped up and came toward us, we altered our courses in many parts of our lives. How strong the wind blew and how wildly the waves crashed varied for each of us. The storm's intensity and damage varied, depending on the circumstances. For some, the storm was a light rain. The water only rippled in the rising wind, thunder rumbled, and lightning struck the sky. At least in part, COVID-19 provided a break for some people: a breather from the rigors of schedules; a chance to rest and reevaluate priorities; an opportunity for a reset.

For others, the pandemic was a tempest raging, with wave after wave of canceled events, furloughed work, isolation orders, and positive test results. Many suffered with long-term effects or even died from the disease.

Then there was the change to our daily lives. Navigating a new normal added stress as countless men and women learned to work from home and keep an even keel for children engaged in remote learning. Undercurrents steadily rose to the surface, as people grew increasingly concerned: how long would stay-at-home orders continue? What protective measures were effective? What would long-term outcomes look like?

For many, life during the COVID-19 crisis felt suspended at best, disrupted for sure, and shipwrecked at worst.

> **R&R:** Recall a portion of your unique situation during the early days of the COVID-19 storm.

PEACE! BE STILL!

What do we know in the sun, in the showers, and in the storm? What can we do when storms rage? Where will we find strength and refuge? Where can we turn when our circumstances spin out of control?

We turn to the One who calms the sea, who steadies us when the waves rage and the winds blow.

We read about raging waves in the Gospel of Mark. Jesus was teaching beside the Sea of Galilee. Such large crowds gathered that He stepped into a boat to speak, while the multitudes sat on the shore to listen. We can imagine Jesus' exhaustion at the end of the day when He told His disciples to take Him to the other side of the sea.

> And a great windstorm arose, and the waves were breaking into the boat, so that the boat was already filling. But [Jesus] was in the stern, asleep on the cushion. And they woke Him and said to Him, "Teacher, do You not care that we are perishing?" And He awoke and rebuked the wind and said to the sea, "Peace! Be still!" And the wind ceased, and there was a great calm. He said to them, "Why are you so afraid? Have you still no faith?" And they were filled with great fear and said to one another, "Who then is this, that even the wind and the sea obey Him?" (Mark 4:37–41)

Jesus commanded the storm to stop with the simple words "Peace! Be still!" (verse 39). The wind and the waves immediately obeyed. The Lord of all creation spoke, and the sea was instantly calm.

May the same silence, obedience, and awe that came over the sea also come over you and me!

DISCUSSION QUESTION 1 What storm was brewing and blowing, aside from the one on the water? (Hint: Take note of the disciples' words to Jesus as they woke Him.) Aside from His exhaustion, what could enable Jesus to sleep through such a storm?

DISCUSSION QUESTION 2 How might Jesus' words have applied to more than just the stormy sea? What does He give us in exchange for our fears as He leads us to trust in Him?

JOURNAL: What one takeaway today enables me to say, "I can be still because I know that He is God"?

DAY 2: PSALM 46: REFUGE IN THE STORM

STUDYING THE PSALM

At the pinnacle of Psalm 46, the Lord proclaims, "Be still, and know that I am God" (Psalm 46:10). The words of this verse are on everything from journals to coffee cups (I own both, by the way). As I write this, I stare at gifts gracing the wall of my home office, reminding me to be still. They are beautiful reminders to stop what I'm doing and be still before the Lord, to know that He is God. (Amen!)

I laughed the other day, however, when I noted some of the literal translations for *be still*: "Stop! Enough!" I wondered how those words would look on the cover of my new journal. We're not misinterpreting this beloved verse when we share it through various visual means, yet there is so much more to take away from it and from the context surrounding it too.

"Be still, and know." Read all of Psalm 46 with these beautiful words in mind. (Note: after we study the full psalm in the first session, we will focus especially on verses 1 and 10, our theme verses, throughout the rest of the study.)

¹God is our refuge and strength, a very present help in trouble.

²Therefore we will not fear though the earth gives way, though the mountains be moved into the heart of the sea,

³though its waters roar and foam, though the mountains tremble at its swelling.

⁴There is a river whose streams make glad the city of God, the holy habitation of the Most High.

⁵God is in the midst of her; she shall not be moved; God will help her when morning dawns.

⁶The nations rage, the kingdoms totter; He utters His voice, the earth melts.

⁷The Lord of hosts is with us; the God of Jacob is our fortress.

[8]Come, behold the works of the LORD, how He has brought desolations on the earth.

[9]He makes wars cease to the end of the earth; He breaks the bow and shatters the spear; He burns the chariots with fire.

[10]"Be still, and know that I am God. I will be exalted among the nations, I will be exalted in the earth!"

[11]The LORD of hosts is with us; the God of Jacob is our fortress.

Let me ask you: If God is our refuge, strength, and very present help (and He is), why does the psalmist sing of cataclysmic disasters and raging nations? Why are these things happening?

The promise of the psalm is not that we will never have troubles; in fact, it implies that we will. Rather, the promise is that God gives us refuge, strength, and help in troubles. His gifts are not dependent upon our circumstances; actually, they far surpass them. Disaster will strike, but we won't need to fear when it does. Isn't that wonderful news?

In the midst of our stormy seasons, we may not be able to say why these things are happening or make sense of our situation, but we can cling to the truth of what we know for certain, as we read in Psalm 46:

❖ God is our refuge: our safe place, stronghold, and shelter. He is our strength; He is mighty to save us from the storm, and He holds us securely in it. He is a very present help amid every trouble. He cannot forsake us, and He will not leave us to battle the storm on our own. The imagery in the verses that follow reveals nature in upheaval and nations raging: the effects of sin in our fallen world.

❖ Whatever the storm, we will not fear, because of who He is (our Refuge) and what He gives us (strength and help). He is with us "though the earth gives way, . . . though its waters roar and foam" (verses 2–3) with every kind of turmoil that may threaten us, body or soul—from hurricanes to cancer, from warring nations to satanic assaults and more.[1]

❖ God is in our midst! "The city of God" (verse 4) has more than one reference point. First it was Jerusalem, where God's people worshiped in His presence in the temple. Second, fulfilling the Scriptures, Jesus is the temple of the living God, and we, by faith, are the new Jerusalem. "In Jesus, God is present for [His] people. He is a help readily found. . . . 'The city of God' no longer names a geographical place but a *people*."[2] Christ lives in us, by faith. Yes, God is in our midst!

DISCUSSION QUESTION 1 Read John 2:18–22. Jesus had just driven moneychangers and sellers from the temple, His Father's house of worship. When He was questioned by the Jewish leaders, what prophetic message did Jesus give concerning Himself? Why couldn't they make sense of it? What is supremely significant for us, as this relates to Psalm 46 and the city of God?

❖ Jesus is the "river whose streams make glad" (Psalm 46:4) by giving life. He is the source of living water (John 4:10–11; 7:38; Revelation 7:17), as we will study in Session 4.

❖ He is all-powerful over all the earth. Even though the nations rage and the mountains tremble, He is in control; He will help His people! He is victorious over every enemy and every threat, natural and man-made. God thunders His wrath against the enemy when "He utters His voice" (verse 6). The Hebrew phrase "when morning dawns" (verse 5) appears in only one other place: Exodus 14:27. "God's deliverance of Israel from Egypt was the central act of salvation in Israel's history. It was when God was most mightily present with them. Remembering it brings comfort and hope for the future."[3] He was their very present help.

DISCUSSION QUESTION 2 Read Exodus 14:27 and the context surrounding it. What happened "when the morning appeared" that revealed God's presence and power? Then compare the similar phrase in Psalm 46:5 and its context. What else is similar? (It may be helpful to note that enemy attacks were most often launched at dawn.)[4] How does this comfort you as you consider personal attacks of the enemy, Satan, today? How are you strengthened as you face the effects of division and unrest in our own nation or the effects of a natural disaster near you?

❖ God is our fortress of protection. He is powerful, immovable. He is with us today and always. "The phrase *with us* constitutes the first part of the name 'Immanuel' ([Isaiah] 7:14)."[5]

❖ He makes wars cease and miraculously brings us peace. "Come, behold" (Psalm 46:8). Come and see God's victory. God is triumphant! We may wonder how we can "come, behold," but we have already beheld Christ's victory at the cross: we have His written Word, filled with personal witnesses, testimonies, and history. We are filled with faith, by the power of the Holy Spirit. With the psalmist, we look ahead to the final victory in the day of Christ's return. Come and see, indeed!

DISCUSSION QUESTION 3 How are the refrains of verses 7 and 11 an echo of verse 1? What does this powerful repetition imply about the psalmist's main purpose in this song of praise?

GOD'S VOICE BREAKS THROUGH: "BE STILL, AND KNOW"

At the pinnacle of the psalm, God's voice breaks through the chaos, the disasters, and the troubles. "Be still" (*rapha*) in Hebrew translates as "to be weak, to let go, to release."[6] It can also mean "stop" or "enough."[7] We stop to hear His voice, to sit in awe of our Savior and know that He is God. He is our strength because we are weak. We acknowledge Him as God of the universe. We release (surrender) our lives to Him, knowing that He is in control and we have no need to fear. When God says, "Be still," it's not a heavy-handed command; it's a grace-filled invitation to be quiet and in awe before the Lord.

By His work, the whole earth—every nation—will one day exalt Him. "Against the idolatry and arrogance of humankind, God has the final say. No other god controls creation and history."[8] The culmination of His work comes in the fulfillment of His promise of salvation: the birth, life, death, resurrection, and return of Jesus. Philippians 2:9–11 proclaims, "God has highly exalted Him and bestowed on Him the name that is above every name, so that at the name of Jesus every knee should bow, in heaven and on earth and under the earth, and every tongue confess that Jesus Christ is Lord, to the glory of God the Father."

> **R&R:** Reflect upon and respond to this sentence from today's reading: When God says, "Be still," it's not a heavy-handed command; it's a grace-filled invitation to be quiet and in awe before the Lord.

Listen for storm language employed by one commentary whose author's summarizing words of Psalm 46 were too powerful not to share:

> A potent antidote to fear in threats of the most dire disaster. The child of God is reminded that God does not lose control, whatever the circumstances may be. Because He has all menacing powers firmly in hand, there is no reason why those who seek *refuge* in Him should not be serene and calm though ominous clouds of disaster darken the sky. Should the universe itself appear to *change* in a cataclysm, causing the mountains to *tremble* and be swallowed up in roaring tidal waves, He still would stand—a bastion of *strength* towering over the seething chaos.[9]

As you've seen already, Jesus is at the heart of Psalm 46; He is the fulfillment of the psalmist's song of praise. He gives us Himself—His power, His presence, and His protection. He provides our ultimate help and hope in the salvation that He won for us at the cross. Envision Jesus praying this psalm in your place before the Father's throne, interceding for you and sharing the praises of your heart from Psalm 46. Because of Jesus' sacrifice, you can approach God's throne too (Hebrews 4:16), confident to ask for everything this psalm promises.[10]

> **R&R:** "God is our refuge and strength, a very present help in trouble" (Psalm 46:1). Apply this verse to your life: in what ways did Jesus fulfill these words of the psalmist for you in a particular storm? Did He calm your storm, or did He calm you, even as the storm still blew?

You and I are swept up in storms of every situation. We may cry out for *release*, praying that He will stop the storm. However, sometimes we receive, instead, *relief*: His strength, calm, and peace as the storm continues to rage. He is in our midst, and therefore, we need not fear.

R&R: "Be still, and know that I am God. I will be exalted among the nations, I will be exalted in the earth" (Psalm 46:10). Ponder a specific storm; maybe it's one you are facing now. How do these words speak to you in your storm? How might Jesus be exalted in your life, through your life, and into your world?

JOURNAL: What one takeaway today enables me to say, "I can be still because I know that He is God"?

DAY 3: OUR H.O.P.E.

CHRIST, OUR ANCHOR, OUR STRONGHOLD IN THE STORM

"Drop anchor!" Even a landlubber like me knows what that means. When the anchor of a sailing ship is lowered, it tethers the vessel to the seabed below, holding it securely in place, immovable. In ancient times, especially during the days of the Early Church, the anchor was a symbol of safety and hope. It's no wonder, then, that Hebrews 6:19 provides an illustration of Christ as our Anchor of hope. It's especially fitting here as we study stormy situations.

Strong and immovable, our Anchor won't let us be swept away by the wind, carried off by a strong current, or capsized. Whether we are encountering a shower or enduring a storm, with the help—the stronghold—of our Savior, we will stay the course.

DISCUSSION QUESTION 1 Read Hebrews 6:19–20. Our hope is anchored in Jesus, who has entered into "the inner place behind the curtain" as our forerunner and on our behalf. (In the temple of Jesus' day, a heavy curtain separated "the inner place" from the rest of the sanctuary. Only the high priest could enter "the inner place" on behalf of the people with the animal sacrifice, as atonement for their sins.) With that backdrop in place, along with a look at Matthew 27:50–51, what do these verses from Hebrews mean?

In every situation, you and I desperately need our Savior, our strength in every storm. Our refuge is in Him. Our help comes from Him. Christ's ultimate purpose was to save us from the tempest, the worst of storms—our sin. Only He, the sinless Son of God, possessed the ability to save all, because all had strayed from the course God had set for His creation. To save us, Christ willingly sank to the greatest depths; He suffered and died in our place to secure our salvation.

Without the strength of Christ holding us fast and keeping us on course, we would drift. We may even be carried away by the waves. We could fall for the ways of the world that may deceive us into believing we can anchor ourselves to the latest cultural doctrine or crafty scheme that could capsize our faith. But we are led by the Holy Spirit, grounded in God's Word, and certain of the hope of salvation we find only in Christ.

DISCUSSION QUESTION 2 Grounded in God's Word, we are strengthened and matured in our faith. What does Ephesians 4:14 tell us regarding that essential growth (using storm imagery to do so)? Write the verse here. Then list current examples of when believers were deceived by human cunning, deceptive doctrine, or another such situation.

Only by faith in Christ can we be saved. In every stormy situation, circumstance, or trial, we cling to this hope; this is the hope we share with a watching world.

> **R&R:** What can you tell a watching world that is drifting, capsizing, or sinking, for lack of the Anchor (not just any anchor, but *the* Anchor), your Savior?

Our hope of eternal life in Christ gives us rock-solid stability. When our storms rage, when the world changes (as it did in unprecedented ways during the COVID-19 pandemic), we can be certain that no situation—no storm—changes God or His purpose. Nothing can remove His stronghold upon us.

In the *Today's Light Devotional Bible*, author Jane Fryar stresses God's unchanging faithfulness, which "gives us hope and courage (Hebrews 6:18). It anchors us, no matter what storms pound hard against our lives. Even if persecution comes for the name of Jesus, we stand on firm ground as we trust His grace toward us."[11] The psalmist speaks of his adversaries attacking him like a "raging wind and tempest" in Psalm 55:8. He finds His shelter in the Lord. Whether our storm comes through persecution, the effects of the coronavirus (or any other illness), temptation that threatens to carry us off or sweep us away, or other trial, we can be still and know that He is God, our Refuge and our strength. He will be exalted over every enemy, every nation, every storm. He holds us steady under the sunniest of skies and in the stormiest of seas.

OVERCOMING THE WORLD

In this world, we will have storms of many kinds. Jesus said we would: "In the world you will have tribulation" (John 16:33). But Jesus didn't stop there. He continued in the very same breath: "But take heart; I have overcome the world." This is the hope that we have in the midst of every stormy circumstance, even those of global proportions: He has overcome the world!

Jesus overcame sin, death, and the power of the devil on our behalf by giving His life and going to hell for us. Then, rising from His grave, He won the victory over death and ascended to the Father in heaven, where He prepares a place for us. With confidence, we await His return. Meanwhile, we view every storm as an opportunity to remember that He is in control and to discover just how strong our Savior is!

DISCUSSION QUESTION 3 Because He has overcome the world, we have this victory too, by faith. What does 1 John 5:4–5 say to confirm this?

He is your H.O.P.E. in the midst of every storm:

Hold: He is your stronghold; He holds you steady, still, immovable.

Overcome: He has overcome sin, death, and the power of the devil, so that you may also overcome, by His grace through faith.

Present: He is with you, now and always. He is present with you in this storm.

Eternity: He is your hope for eternity, now and forever; He has promised you eternal life with Him.

SEPARATION, BUT NOT FROM GOD

During the COVID-19 pandemic, I was filled with H.O.P.E. thanks to the words of several godly people, including a dear sister in Christ, Debbie (national president of the Lutheran Women's Missionary League). She wrote:

As we deal with the cancellation of many events, we feel like we are losing control of our lives. If that's how you are feeling, then I suggest you pick up the Bible and read. We have never been in control of our lives, and I thank God for that truth! Our Lord has been and remains in control. . . .

Let's not look at our confinement—let's look to the cross for what true separation was like for our Savior as He hung on the cross for our sins. Let's not look at the stock market and despair—let's look to the empty grave and find joy in the treasure of heaven.

We've been asked to isolate ourselves from others for our safety and theirs. God assures us we are never separated from His love.[12]

Who shall separate us from the love of Christ? Shall tribulation, or distress, or persecution, or famine, or nakedness, or danger, or sword? . . . For I am sure that neither death nor life, nor angels nor rulers, nor things present nor things to come, nor powers, nor height nor depth, nor anything else in all creation, will be able to separate us from the love of God in Christ Jesus our Lord. (Romans 8:35, 38–39)

The best thing we can do when battered by a storm is to trust in the One who holds us still. We can trust Him to use every circumstance for good—for His purpose. During my daughter's time of social separation amid the COVID-19 storm, she wrote:

> I go on walks each day and watch. A large family plays kickball in the park. A mother and daughter go on a run together. More people are out in this (already active) neighborhood than ever before, smiling and nodding at one another like this tiny human interaction is a lifeline. I can't help but feel like our priorities are resetting. We are becoming! We're spending time where it matters, and we are valuing the formerly mundane, and it feels so, so good.[13]

Courtney saw, already, some good that God was working through her situation, and it gave her hope. Are our eyes looking for the good that God is doing, even in a storm?

R&R: Write Romans 8:28 on a sticky note in a location where you'll receive a daily reminder. Commit the verse to memory. You are indeed called according to His purpose!

R&R: Name a time (or several) when you saw God work all things together for good. How did it fill you with hope? Where do you see some of the ways God may be using a stormy situation today?

JOURNAL: What one takeaway today enables me to say, "I can be still because I know that He is God"?

DAY 4: TRUSTING HIM IN THE STORM

IS GOD DISTANT?

When I'm struggling, I am tempted to think that God is distant. Maybe I don't feel His presence. But that doesn't negate the truth that He is present. He is not just near me—He is here with me! I am not defeated or destroyed. He is fighting my battle with me and often for me without my help. Just because I don't receive a certain answer at a specific time or according to my wishes doesn't mean He isn't faithful to hear. He is always faithful. His provision may look different than I envisioned it would, and so I may fail to recognize it for what it is. Not only is His vision perfect, but it is also limitless. He sees the storms I face today and the sun that shines tomorrow or the next day. If not yet then, for certain in eternity. So I place my trust in Him.

DISCUSSION QUESTION 1 You and I can cry out with the same confidence as the psalmist: "But You, O Lord, do not be far off! O You my help, come quickly to my aid!" (Psalm 22:19). We place our trust in Him. As God's people faced enemy armies, faithful leaders such as Joshua, King David, and King Jehoshaphat trusted Him too. What do you hear in these verses, regarding God's presence and help? Your battles and storms may be vastly different, but how do these reassurances and reminders apply to you too?

- Joshua 1:9: The Lord speaks to Joshua.

- Psalm 16:8: King David speaks, as inspired by the Lord.

- 2 Chronicles 20:17: A Levite priest, by the Spirit of the Lord, speaks before King Jehoshaphat and the people.

TOP TEN

Karen Sue, my friend and fellow blogger, encouraged many people through the words she shared during the COVID-19 pandemic and at a time of great tension and unrest in our nation. She had faith in God to use this unprecedented time for good, to bring about greater trust and courage in His people. She even titled her blog series "Courage through the COVID-19 Storm." (Yes, *storm.*) She wrote several posts about healthy actions people could take, with God's help, and in response to His great grace for them.

R&R: Following are the top ten tips from my friend's posts. Read the corresponding verses for each tip. Look over the list and challenge yourself to one action per day, creating a simple implementation plan. Remember God's grace as you go, and give yourself some grace too. Trust Him to work through His Word in your life today. Extend this challenge to others as well.

1. Be thankful (1 Thessalonians 5:16–18).

2. Go outside (Psalm 121:1–3; see also Psalm 92:4; 111:2).

3. Think healthy thoughts (Philippians 4:8).

4. Live today; do not worry about tomorrow (Matthew 6:34).

5. Keep your eyes on God (Romans 14:8; see also Hebrews 12:2).

6. Stay active (see 1 Timothy 4:8).

7. Have realistic expectations (see 1 Timothy 6:6–8).

8. Laugh—the more, the better (see Psalm 126:2; Proverbs 15:13).

9. Be kind (Colossians 3:12).

10. Apologize (Philippians 4:5; see also Ephesians 4:32).[14]

TRUST IN THE LORD

My friend Carol recalled growing in trust too:

> Many things were weighing heavily on my heart. . . . Personal challenges and difficulties born of everyday life. In response to these feelings of overwhelmingness, I cried out to the Lord: "Lord, I just don't see a pathway through this!" And immediately, He gently replied to my struggling heart: "Carol, trust Me."
>
> My go-to verses in life [are] Proverbs 3:5–6, "Trust in the LORD with all your heart, and do not lean on your own understanding. In all your ways

acknowledge Him, and He will make straight your paths". . . . I've clung to [these verses] ever since that time and they have given me peace and joy despite the circumstances that swirl around me. Now again, I have the opportunity to stand firmly within these verses' power and truth.

Simply put, I've been given another opportunity to trust God.

• Trust that He is who He says He is.

• Trust that His understanding is significantly greater than mine.

• Trust that His promises ring true no matter what is going on around me.

• Trust that when I can't see the path up ahead [sometimes due to the storm itself], that He not only sees it but is also laying it down ahead of me.

• Trust that when I lean on Him instead of on my own strength, that I am steady and secure for my travels.[15]

> **R&R:** With what do you need to trust God today? He is with you and ready to respond to whatever is weighing on your heart. Rest in His forgiveness for past and present failures, confident that you can trust Him for the journey ahead.

IS CHANGE AN IDENTITY THIEF?

Maybe our stormy situation has been all about change. At one time, we thought we were secure, anchoring ourselves to roles of mother, wife, professional, teacher, volunteer, or whatever our vocation. Then a tidal wave of change swept in and knocked our feet out from under us, wiping out the world of security we had built around ourselves. The active mom no longer had a purpose, because her children grew up and moved away. The "wife" label didn't apply when there was no husband in the house anymore. The "professional, employee, teacher" title evaporated with a layoff or retirement. Now we are unsure of our identity. It feels as though change has stolen it, eroding our sense of purpose in the process.

Nevertheless, we can trust our unchanging Lord when He says that *who* we are, first and foremost, is really a matter of *whose* we are. We belong to Him.

No matter what happens in life, regardless of our circumstances or how our roles change, our identity cannot be stolen because it is rooted in the One who redeems us, restores us, and loves us immeasurably more than we can grasp: "[I pray] that you, being rooted and grounded in love, may have strength to comprehend with all the saints what is the breadth and length and height and depth, and to know the love of Christ that surpasses knowledge, that you may be filled with all the fullness of God" (Ephesians 3:17–19).

DISCUSSION QUESTION 2 Your identity is rooted in Christ. In what does the Ephesians passage say you are rooted? How are they one and the same? Note the four-directional scope of the limitless love of Christ. What is significant about it?

DISCUSSION QUESTION 3 Your unchanging identity is found and centered in Christ. What does the One who created and formed you have to say to you in Isaiah 43:1–2?

"Fear not, _____."

Circle the words that define you. Note the imagery. To what could you liken these storms of nature? Where is God in them?

JOURNAL: What one takeaway today enables me to say, "I can be still because I know that He is God"?

DAY 5: RELIEF OR RELEASE

BY HIS POWER, NOT OUR OWN

Maybe your current situation looks different from those I've mentioned so far. Or maybe you can relate to each of them on some level. Regardless, you may feel helpless in your unique situation.

Maybe it's an opportunity that you were certain would come your way but hasn't. Perhaps it's a need you are unable to fill, or it could be a crisis you can't solve.

Discouraged, you may even feel like giving up because you've come to realize that there is nothing you can do to fix or change this situation—at least, not now. That's an especially hard pill to swallow, because you would like to think you can make it all better. After all, you've heard comments such as these: "If it is to be, it's up to me." "If you can see it, you can achieve it." "She believed she could, and so she did." Deceptive at best and flat-out false at worst, these sayings feed a desire for that fleeting thing called *control*.

> **R&R:** Have you heard similar sayings, made popular by modern claims of control? What are they? How do you guard yourself against falling for them?

Maybe this situation has made it clear that you don't have control. In fact, it has proven your powerlessness. While you would desperately like things to be different, consider this: God may have allowed this place, this time, and this situation to help you see your need for Him. You can't go it alone, especially not in this _____ *(fill in the blank)*_____ situation. He meets you where you are: helpless, discouraged, or disappointed. Trust Him to hold you steady through your storm and give you relief in it; trust Him also to bring you through and provide release from it. Don't park yourself in a place of doubt or discouragement; rather, let God's power enable you to rise above it and press on in His strength.

DISCUSSION QUESTION 1 Read the apostle Paul's empowering words in Philippians 3:13–14. As you "[strain] forward," what lies ahead? God has called you, according to His purposes, in Christ. How does knowing your calling impact your desire to press on, even in a storm or when you feel helpless?

In your helplessness, God provides strength through His Word. He is the help to the helpless; He does all that you cannot. Listen to His counsel. Cry out with your complaints. Pour out your heart in prayer. Call on God in the midst of your storms. He hears; He answers. You can trust that His answers are best for you. They bring Him glory, and they further His kingdom (whether or not you recognize them in the moment). Your helplessness can become the posture and perspective from which you see your need for God's strength and recognize your own reception of His grace.

SUMMER CAMP IN A CORONAVIRUS STORM

We often fail to understand the ways and the whys of God. My friend Katie's candid words reflect her whys—and her faith—during her summer storm, when she cried out with her complaints and received an unexpected answer. Katie shared with me personally:

> I have gone to Camp Luther of Nebraska ever since I was little. [For years, I've dreamed of becoming a summer camp counselor, so I applied in 2020.] I received the position and was so excited to work at camp. I have loved leading mission trips and leading Vacation Bible School, so I was looking forward to spreading God's Word at one of my favorite places!

> We all know how our "friend" COVID-19 ruined all of our spring and summer plans in 2020. I received the news that Camp Luther would not be opening for youth camps. I asked God, "Why? Why would You allow this? You have the power to stop this virus and put children out at camp to learn Your Word. Then I would be able to have a wonderful summer growing closer to You too." In that tough time of uncertainty and disappointment, it was hard to be still and know that God is God. I had no idea what God was doing in all of this, but I can say with confidence that He had a plan. His plans are bigger than ours and His thoughts are higher than our thoughts [Isaiah 55:8–9].

> Because youth camps were closed, Camp Luther had to turn away more than half of the counselors. . . . God definitely answered my prayer. I had prayed that God would still use me in some way at camp that summer, and He answered my prayer. I was surprised to learn that I would be doing some maintenance work instead of serving as a counselor, but I was just happy that I would still get to be there and serve.[16]

Katie kept a journal during her summer journey and shared this with me too:

I have seen God working through me this summer as I have interacted with families, but I have also learned that my behind-the-scenes maintenance role is also very important. Even though maintenance doesn't feel like the ministry of leading a campfire, it is still something that takes a servant heart. I have learned that my spirit is willing, but my flesh is so weak. I can't do anything that I do here on my own—I have to fully rely on God. And He remains faithful. A few times I have found myself questioning why I am here, and I keep going back to the fact that God called me here. He brought me here because He knew I could fulfill this job, even though I don't always believe I can every day. But I can trust that God has a plan for me to carry out this summer.[17]

God knows what He is doing, even when we don't. His promises still stand; great is His faithfulness.

DISCUSSION QUESTION 2 Katie listened to the Lord's counsel, trusting His Word. Open your Bible to Isaiah 55:8–9 and hear God speak these words to you too. How did God choose to answer Katie's cries? Was it in the ways she had hoped? How can you see that His answers were best for her? How did they bring Him glory and further His kingdom?

WHY, LORD?

Not every storm story ends as Katie's did. This side of heaven, we may not understand the reason for every stormy situation or the ways God is working, but we can take heart that Jesus, our Savior, is our Refuge and Strength in them; He is our Help throughout them. The prophet Isaiah echoes the psalmist: "Fear not, for I am with you; be not dismayed, for I am your God; I will strengthen you, I will help you, I will uphold you with My righteous right hand" (Isaiah 41:10).

DISCUSSION QUESTION 3 Name all the ways Isaiah 41:10 echoes portions of Psalm 46, if not with the same word or phrase, then with a similar meaning. Enjoy greater understanding as you compare like passages and bask in God's promises.

> **R&R:** When and how has God been a refuge in a particular storm in your life? How has He changed your situation? How has He changed you, by His grace? How did He provide *release* from the storm or *relief* for you in the storm, helping you to grow in His grace?

R&R: Recall one difficult or challenging situation that ended up helping you to grow and reinforced your faith. What might be different for you today if you had never faced that difficulty or challenge?

Whatever your stormy situation, place these guides before you:

❖ God's Word: Receive truth to which you can cling, strength from the Holy Spirit, and the best kind of encouragement from the One who is always with you.

❖ People: Surround yourself with fellow believers who will point you to His truth. They may be the conduit of God's strength in many situations.

❖ Mementos or memories: Reminders of God's past and present provision will go a long way to encourage you as you face a storm.

R&R: "God is our refuge and strength, a very present help in trouble" (Psalm 46:1). In light of all you've learned in this week's session, describe how Jesus fulfills these words of the psalmist for you. What does His *relief* in the storm or *release* from the storm mean to you?

He is with you in the midst of every storm, to guide and protect, to calm and bless, and to provide peace in His presence. Seek Him in your storm.

JOURNAL: What one takeaway today enables me to say, "I can be still because I know that He is God"?

VIEWER GUIDE

SESSION 1: STORMY SITUATIONS

READ MARK 4:35–41.

"Windstorm" (Mark 4:37), from the Greek *lailaps*: _____
_____.

Jesus has been faithfully _____ _____ _____ and faithful to _____, all along.

With the Lord's help, how can you respond to every stormy situation? How can you "be still, and know that [He is] God"? How can you know that He has you in His grip, even in the storm?

1. Seek out His _____.

2. Take your fear and your storm to Him in _____.

3. _____ into the face of Jesus!

You and I are swept up in storms of every _____. We may cry out for _____ (hoping He will stop the storm), but sometimes we receive, instead, _____ (His strength, calm, and peace), even as the storm continues to rage.

DISCUSS

> God is our refuge and strength, a very present help in trouble. Therefore we will not fear though the earth gives way, though the mountains be moved into the heart of the sea, though its waters roar and foam, though the mountains tremble at its swelling. . . . "Be still, and know that I am God." (Psalm 46:1–3, 10)

As you consider one or more stormy situations, what do your roaring waters and trembling mountains look like? How is your storm brewing or blowing in a specific situation? What trouble has come because of this storm?

Can you see God working to calm you or calm the storm, helping you to trust Him in it? How do you know that He is God and R.E.S.T. (*refuge*, *ever*-present *strength* in *trouble*) in that truth? How or where do you see His help?

READY TO R.E.S.T.?

READ AND REFLECT: What do the Scriptures and this Bible study say about stormy situations? What do they say about Jesus, your refuge in these storms? What were your biggest takeaways?

EXAMINE QUESTIONS AND EXPLORE ANSWERS: For greater understanding and for application, seek answers in Scripture and meditate upon the personal questions.

SHARE: Tell about your takeaways and your storm, with a group or alone, as you write or pray about them.

TRUST your Refuge, the One who provides *relief* in the storm or *release* from it.

THE STORM OF SIN

THE WOMAN CAUGHT IN ADULTERY— JOHN 8:2–11

DAY 1: WRITING IN THE SAND

WORDS IN THE SAND

I stood alone on the beach at sunrise, in the middle of a women's retreat. I'd walked the same beach with a friend the evening before, writing words in the sand, scooping the sand into my hands and letting it trickle through my fingers. Mindful of God's presence that evening, my thoughts had turned to Jesus and His encounter with the woman caught in adultery. What had He written in the sand that day, as the guilty woman's accusers waited for His verdict? What were His thoughts toward her?

Then I wondered what He would write regarding my guilt. What are His thoughts toward me? Am I swept away in the storm of my sins, as this woman had been in hers? Have I justified any of my actions or become trapped by them? I know that I stand guilty and condemned. What would His verdict be? What was His verdict of her?

A WOMAN'S STORM OF SIN—BASED ON JOHN 8:2–11

A clamor of thundering footsteps and a roar of angry voices approached her hideaway with the man she had been seeing in secret. Religious leaders burst into the bedroom, finding her compromised. She scrambled to cover herself, even as they grabbed her by the arms and dragged her with them to the temple court.

A mere object to the religious leaders who accused her, the woman would soon learn she was a convenient casualty for their evil scheme. But she also knew she was guilty. She had dishonored the sacred gift of marriage and broken the law of her people. The whirling, swirling storm of her sin had swept her up and carried her away, straight into her lover's arms.

Ashamed, she hung her head and felt the tears flowing down her face, even as she was led toward the temple courtyard. She barely felt the sharp sting of their grip on her arms as they pushed through the crowd that had gathered that morning. Someone was there teaching; she could hear His voice. Was it the One her people were all talking about? The shouts of the religious leaders caused a commotion in the crowd, and the speaker stopped. She was a public spectacle, though she dared not look up to see the angry faces of her accusers or the stones they clutched. Trembling, she could almost feel the glares from the crowd, as they judged her and muttered to one another. The religious leaders shoved her in front of the crowd, then called out to the One who was teaching that day, their tone anything but respectful. To this man and all who were assembled, they announced the charge against her: adultery. According to the law, she should be put to death.

But why ask this Teacher to comment? What kind of authority did they believe Him to have, that they wanted His ruling on the matter? What difference would it make anyway? The law was the law. Still, the leaders leaned in, maliciously eager for His reply.

The Teacher said nothing. Instead, He bent down and wrote with His finger on the ground. Yet they persisted until He stood. Staring at them, and then motioning to her, the Teacher—Jesus—said, "Let him who is without sin among you be the first to throw a stone at her" (verse 7).

Silence. Jesus bent down again and wrote on the ground. Though the woman could not bring herself to see what He wrote, she was baffled by His response. One by one, the religious leaders loosened their grip on the stones and turned to leave. The woman heard muffled thuds as one stone after another hit the ground.

When she looked up at last, she watched the religious leaders look from Jesus to the ground, defeated. Shoulders slumped, they walked away—the elders first and the younger ones behind them, either convicted or ashamed. Before long, every accuser was gone.

Jesus stood and said to her, "Woman, where are they? Has no one condemned you?" (verse 10).

Finding her voice to answer His question, she spoke for the first time. "No one, Lord" (verse 11), she whispered, cautiously looking into His face. His soft smile matched the compassion in His voice: "Neither do I condemn you; go, and from now on sin no more" (verse 11).

That day, a dark storm cloud lifted from this woman as she took her first step into the light of freedom—of new life! Hearing Jesus' words of forgiveness over and over in her mind, she felt the weight of condemnation lift: the sentence for her sin was removed. Formerly guilty and trapped, she was forgiven and freed, given the undeserved gift of grace! She received new life in Him.

> **R&R:** Pause to ponder the story of this woman's storm, also reading John 8:2–11; then write what stood out to you. What was your first and immediate takeaway?

DISCUSSION QUESTION 1 "God is our refuge and strength, a very present help in trouble" (Psalm 46:1). In what ways did Jesus fulfill the words of the psalmist for this woman? How was He her refuge in her storm of sin?

DISCUSSION QUESTION 2 "Be still, and know that I am God. I will be exalted among the nations, I will be exalted in the earth!" (Psalm 46:10). Picture this woman's life following her encounter with Christ. She may have even known these words of the psalmist. How do you think they would have spoken to her? How may Jesus have been exalted in her life (and in her world, through her) from that day forward?

Maybe this woman's story leads you to consider your own. What storms of sin have swept you up and carried you away? Maybe you have struggled with gossip, jealousy, or hate; maybe you've battled a weakness with sexual sin, addiction, selfishness, or something else. Know that you are not alone in your storm, nor are you helpless against its power over you because of the One who is with you. Maybe you're still in the storm, but thanks to Jesus, your Strength, your helper, and your Refuge, you can trust that the dark storm clouds will lift one day, here or in eternity.

- Already, you have Jesus' words of forgiveness as you confess your sins to Him.

- Already, the condemnation for your sin has lifted and the sentence has been removed. Christ took it from you at the cross.

- Already, you stand in the light of freedom by faith, God's gift to you!

Be still, and know that He is God, incomparably more powerful than your storm and your struggle with your sin. You do not need to fear "though the earth gives way, though the mountains be moved into the heart of the sea" (Psalm 46:2).

> **R&R:** Write about a storm of sin with which you have struggled or battled. Come to the Lord, confessing your sin and seeking His help, confident of the forgiveness you receive in Christ.

WORDS IN THE SAND, REVISITED

There I stood, on the beach at sunrise. While I couldn't pretend to know what Jesus had written in the sand that day, I could imagine what He wrote, based on His beautiful, grace-filled response to the woman caught in her storm. I am given a glimpse across Scripture of His countless thoughts for me, and I marvel at them, just as the psalmist did: "How precious to me are Your thoughts, O God! How vast is the sum of them! If I would count them, they are more than the sand" (Psalm 139:17–18a).

Just as in the evening before, I was again mindful of God's continued presence and His innumerable thoughts: "I awake, and I am still with You" (verse 18b).

The mind of God, the meaning of His words for me, and the depth of His grace are beyond my full comprehension. Like the psalmist, I marvel as I contemplate the vastness of God's thoughts. His thoughts of me. Little old me. Little old sinful me.

He has searched me and known me (Psalm 139:1). He knows a word before it is on my tongue (verse 4). There is nowhere I can flee from His presence (verse 7). He knit me together in my mother's womb (verse 13). His works are wonderful (verse 14).

How precious to me are His thoughts. The sum of them is more than the sand.

I couldn't even count the number of grains that trickled through my fingers the evening before. And now, at sunrise, I took in the breadth of the beach, the expanse of sand before my eyes. A storm had come in the night and washed my words away. I smiled, knowing my sins had been washed away too, but His words of grace for me remain. Right there and then, in the stillness at sunrise, I lifted my hands and praised my Lord, my Creator, Savior, and Comforter! "How precious to me are Your thoughts, O God!" (verse 17).

R&R: Do you know the thoughts He has for you? Read Psalm 139:1–18. How precious, indeed! What verse or verses cause your jaw to drop in wonder of His mindfulness of you? Why? Be still before the Lord as you rest in this truth.

JOURNAL: What one takeaway today enables me to say, "I can be still because I know that He is God"?

DAY 2: CAUGHT IN A STORM

SITTING IN A STORM

Most of us can say we've been caught in a weather storm. We can probably share details as if it were yesterday. Maybe the storm cropped up out of nowhere, such as the flash flood I shared in the last session, or maybe it was in the forecast but we ignored it or misgauged where or when it would strike. Regardless, we were caught in it.

When I was a little girl, I was nearly caught in a tornado. My mom was on the phone with neighbors who could see it coming. She had called her three daughters to the basement, but I chose not to listen and headed outside instead. I pretended that I was protecting Drowsy, my baby doll. The wind blew wildly as I wrapped Drowsy in her blanket and held her close, seated on the concrete-topped cistern in our yard. I was her strong protector. Did I think I was stronger than the storm? Did I not realize the scope of it? Did I fail to see the danger in which I'd placed myself or the disobedience of my daring choice? Just before the storm could grab me and carry me away, my mom came for me, saved me, and sent me to safety. (You can believe she made sure I would never sit in a storm again!)

The Lord calls us by His Word, but sometimes we choose not to listen and we go another way.

- We may sit in the storm of our sin, thinking we are strong enough to withstand it or overcome it on our own.

- We might listen for the roar of thunder and seek the lightning strike, moving toward them even though they warn that something worse is on its way.

- Sometimes we blast straight into a storm, naive of its scope or the dangers of succumbing to it.

- We may deny we're stuck in a storm because we don't want to let go of the sin causing it.

DISCUSSION QUESTION 1 If my storm story reminded you of one of your own, write about it or share it with others. If any of the scenarios above speak to you, circle them. Beside the ones you circled, write how you can take action, by God's grace and with His help, to respond differently. (For instance, when the Lord calls us by His Word, we can confess our sins, listen, learn, and follow Him.)

The religious elite accused a woman caught in a storm of adultery. Maybe she knew the law but willfully defied it. It's entirely possible that the woman was, instead, a victim of sexual crimes committed against her. Maybe she sought the attention and affection of the wrong man too many times. Or just maybe she was so used to living this way that she didn't think her life could be different. Regardless, she was caught, grabbed, and carried away by her accusers charging her with her crime.[18] The religious leaders were less concerned with making sure she was lawfully punished for her crime than with using her as a pawn in their latest move against Jesus. With ulterior motives, they hoped to trap Jesus with His own words to establish a basis for arrestable accusations against Him.

DISCUSSION QUESTION 2 Sin comes in many forms and storms. The woman was caught up in her sin, and then caught in it. But what about the religious leaders who caught her? In what storms of sin were they involved?

DISCUSSION QUESTION 3 We know little about the woman, but we can conclude she was a Jew because she lived under the same Mosaic Law as the Pharisees. What might have been her perception of God, of her people's religion, and of its treatment of sin, as a result of her treatment by its leaders? How does this remind you of the perceptions of some people today whose family's belief system is guided only by God's Law? What might happen when these same people are caught in a storm of sin?

GUILTY!

The woman's understanding of her people's religion would most likely have stemmed from the very leaders who condemned her. They were the teachers of the Law, after all, and dictated the Jewish people's beliefs and practices. Their misguided, self-righteous piety overrode any compassion or concern they may have had for her or others. Sadly, their ceremonial lip service and outward attention to every letter of the Law (through which they thought they had favor with God) could not negate the guilt of their own sin within them. They practiced the Law but rejected the Gospel message that Jesus brought to them.

DISCUSSION QUESTION 4 Both people who engaged in the act of adultery had committed the crime. So where was the woman's partner, the man with whom she had been caught in this crime of passion? Do you think she was set up? Was this an example of a double standard being played out? While we can suppose some things, what do we know it was?

Clearly, the woman was guilty—caught in the act. But the unfairness of the situation stirs feelings of compassion within me. Maybe it does with you too. After all, making her stand as a spectacle in front of Jesus and the crowd was an unnecessary act of humiliation, as these men could have held her in custody while making their appeal to Jesus.[19] A barrage of accusations was thrown at her, although a single stone had not yet been hurled.

DISCUSSION QUESTION 5 If the religious leaders' intent was to uphold the Law, what was wrong with this picture? Turn to Leviticus 20:10 and Deuteronomy 22:22. According to Mosaic Law, who was guilty of adultery, and what punishment were they to receive?

ACCORDING TO THE LAW

The situation presented a potential conflict for Jesus. Mosaic Law prescribed death as punishment for the act of adultery, but Roman law did not. To uphold one would put Jesus in conflict with the other. In the religious leaders' minds, Jesus could not avoid entrapment, which was just what they wanted. "If Jesus called for the stoning, he would violate Roman law, which reserved capital punishment for the Romans to execute. If Jesus said, 'Let the woman go,' He would violate Mosaic Law."[20]

Mosaic Law also commanded utter honesty of an accuser. If the testimony of witnesses included false motives or a false statement, they would have blood on their hands and the same punishment could be placed upon them (Deuteronomy 19:18–19). The Pharisees altered the Law of Moses for their own purpose and plot. They had created their own storm.

> **R&R:** Let's admit it. We too have altered facts (or disobeyed God's Law) for our own misguided purposes. When have you created this particular kind of storm? What was your motive for doing so? (Was it to win an argument? stay out of trouble? gain the upper hand?) Confess these storms of your own making, and trust in God's full and complete forgiveness in Christ. Take time for a prayer of confession, knowing that as you pray, you have God's forgiveness through Jesus.

Today's topics make us wince because they speak to our sad state as a sinner. If we're honest, we can see ourselves in the woman and in the Pharisees. Caught in so many storms of sin, you and I are guilty as charged. We break God's Law. We cannot keep it on our own. But—praise God—we are not on our own! The Good News of the Gospel is ours in Jesus, who took our guilt and condemnation upon Himself at the cross and removed them from us completely and for eternity, "as far as the east is from the west" (Psalm 103:12).

The Law shows us our sin. Jesus fulfilled the Law for us. The Gospel shows us our Savior.

"If we say we have no sin, we deceive ourselves, and the truth is not in us. If we confess our sins, He is faithful and just to forgive us our sins and to cleanse us from all unrighteousness" (1 John 1:8–9). Confess your sins to God, confident of His refuge for you in Christ, found in His redemption for you! You are cleansed, forgiven, and free!

DISCUSSION QUESTION 6 Read Romans 3:23–24 and write it here: _____

_____

_____

_____.

Do you see the clear and careful distinction of Law and Gospel in these verses? What words do you find most comforting?

JOURNAL: What one takeaway today enables me to say, "I can be still because I know that He is God"?

DAY 3: REDEEMED!

CAN I HAVE A DO-OVER?

Have you ever wished for a do-over? I know I have. Immediately after a regrettable action, you would give anything to undo that foolish, poor, or misguided thing you did. Maybe you envision erasing the board. Deleting the scene. Cleaning the slate. In your head, you play out the scene differently, undoing the damage by undoing the deed, if that were possible. But it's not, and now you face condemnation. Maybe your friends have scattered and your enemies are gloating. You're certain that some people are scrutinizing, criticizing, or gossiping about you. Some may even begin to define you by your mistake.

> **R&R:** Consider a time when others caught you in a specific sin or learned about it. How did you feel? What was their reaction? Did they condemn you, call you out, or show you grace? How? Prayerfully consider how you can respond if you are faced by accusers today, knowing that God has already flung their accusations away from you, forgiving and redeeming you in Christ.

Maybe the accused woman envisioned a do-over as she stood in shame before Jesus. If she had friends nearby, perhaps they scattered, or like her enemies, they gloated. The crowd likely leaned in, scrutinizing the situation and her. Even today we define her by her sin: "the woman caught in adultery."

DISCUSSION QUESTION 1 Though this unnamed woman is defined by her sin, we know the whole story and how it ends. What phrases could we use to define her better? Are you defined by your sin? What words do you think the Lord would give you, redeemed and chosen in Him?

When Jesus knelt to write in the sand, the woman may have thought He was inscribing her sin and her sentence, making it official. While the words would eventually blow away, she would have believed her record would be anything but clean. Do you wonder what Jesus wrote in the sand that day? While no one knows what He inscribed, we know that Scripture uses the Greek word *grapho*, which refers to letters or words.[21] He wasn't merely drawing or doodling. "Sometimes judges wrote down their sentence before pronouncing it."[22] Some have surmised that Jesus was actually writing the names and sins of the woman's accusers who hovered over her that day, and not her own. He could have been listing the Commandments, reminding the

Pharisees of the entire Law, not just the portion they had picked out and twisted for their evil purposes.[23]

JESUS' BRILLIANT PLAY

Jesus turned their own game back on them with His brilliant play. Since Mosaic Law also called for witnesses to be the first to carry out the death sentence (Deuteronomy 17:7), Jesus made His move, calling out their hate and hypocrisy by saying, in so many words, "Go ahead and do your job—that is, if you are without sin." It's important to note that Jesus wasn't specifying only one type of sin as He challenged them with His words. "The phrase is quite general and means 'without any sin,' not 'without this sin.' "[24]

Maybe Jesus' words struck a chord. While the religious leaders considered themselves self-righteous, they probably knew they were being called out. They had turned Judaism into a religion of rules, outwardly observing every letter of Mosaic Law and adding hundreds of man-made commands. Inwardly, however, they were "full of greed and self-indulgence" (Matthew 23:25, a portion of Jesus' seven woes against the teachers of the law, whom He called hypocrites). They considered themselves clean according to the Law and made it their duty to judge anyone found in violation of it. Jesus revealed their hypocrisy.

THE JUDGMENT SEAT

This story reminds me that at times I have also placed myself in the judgment seat of someone else, while living out the misguided motto "Do as I say, not as I do." Even if I do as I ought, my heart might not be in it. Either way, I practice hypocrisy when I judge others for their sin while ignoring or justifying my own.

DISCUSSION QUESTION 2 Are you sitting in judgment of someone for his or her sins? Is that the same as recognizing sin and calling it out? Look at Matthew 7:1–5. What does Jesus say here, concerning our own sin and the sins of others? What should motivate our response to someone struggling with sin?

TEACHABLE MOMENTS

Jesus' carefully calculated responses, first to the Pharisees and then to the woman, started as He knelt to write in the sand and followed with strong words regarding sin. To both, He was teaching; to both, He was providing an opportunity to acknowledge and turn from sin.

DISCUSSION QUESTION 3 Read again John 8:6–11. Consider Jesus' teachable moments and His compassionate opportunity for each party. Twice He writes in the sand. Twice He speaks. Knowing what we do about the Pharisees' hearts and motives, what do Jesus' responses say about the extent of His love for all people?

After the Pharisees heard Jesus' response, they walked away, the oldest ones first. "Elders would have had a greater share of responsibility and provided leadership for the rest."[25] How fitting that the very people who came to shame another ended up leaving in shame.

Jesus didn't minimize or excuse either party's sins. God's Word, from Mosaic Law to the words of Christ, makes clear the judgment that comes with sin. Judgment is rightfully God's—and God's alone—to make. His judgment was placed squarely on Christ, who received full condemnation for the sins of the world. The Lord calls people to repentance. With compassion, He gives us the same opportunity to acknowledge and turn from our sin too.

DISCUSSION QUESTION 4 Read 2 Peter 3:9. Write in your own words God's desire—His heart—for all people. Since this is true, why aren't all people saved?

FREE INDEED!

The Pharisees sought only to condemn. Jesus sought to bring sinners to repentance. While the Pharisees wanted to destroy Jesus—and a woman along the way—God desired to redeem His people through Jesus.

Suddenly, the woman no longer faced the condemnation of the Pharisees. Suddenly, she stood alone with Christ. (While the crowd remained, they could not accuse her, since they had not witnessed her crime; those who brought the charge were gone.) Perhaps self-condemnation still consumed her. She was incapable of excusing her very apparent sin and unable to remove it or pay for it. Nothing could earn her forgiveness. Then Jesus said it: "Neither do I condemn you" (John 8:11). Jesus gave her what neither the Pharisees nor she could ever earn or deserve. He gave her grace.

Jesus addressed her as "woman" (verse 10; Greek *gynê*), in kindness and favor and with respect.[26] In His response, "Neither do I condemn you" (verse 11), He proclaimed to her the purpose for which He had come: "For God did not send His Son into the world to condemn the world, but in order that the world might be saved through Him" (John 3:17).

DISCUSSION QUESTION 5 How does Jesus' compassionate response to the woman impact your understanding of His response when He or others catch you in the act of any sin, for which you are remorseful? Read 1 John 1:8–9.

What had the people witnessed thus far that day? Pious acts could not remove or negate sin. Everyone, from the self-righteous religious rulers to the adulterous woman to the crowds in the temple, deserved a death sentence for their sins. No sinner could perform, earn, or act his or her way toward righteousness. It was—and is—a free gift, by God's grace through faith in Christ.

I'll say it again: we've been caught, time after time, in our own storms of sin. We are undeniably guilty. Our sins condemn us. Maybe people condemn us too. Jesus is just as personal with each of us as He was with the woman caught in her sin. He meets us right where we stand. He knows our sorry hearts. He looks upon us with compassion and says, "I do not condemn you"; "your sins are forgiven" (Luke 7:48). Just as we were once completely guilty, we are now completely pardoned. Don't let others' condemning words, opinions, or actions hold you hostage. Jesus forgives and frees!

> **R&R:** Finish writing Jesus' words in John 8:36: "If the Son sets you free, ＿＿＿
> ＿＿＿＿＿＿＿＿＿＿＿＿＿＿＿＿＿＿＿＿＿＿＿＿＿＿＿＿＿＿." Free from
> the tumult of the storm, you can be still and know: He is God, your Savior
> from the storm of sin; your refuge is found in His redemption. Take a quiet
> moment now to whisper the words of this verse a few times, reflecting on
> them as you receive them, trusting the One who is your refuge.

JOURNAL: What one takeaway today enables me to say, "I can be still because I know that He is God"?

DAY 4: GO AND SIN NO MORE

BAGGAGE CLAIM

Have you ever stood at an airport's baggage claim and watched other travelers while waiting for your luggage? I have.

Following a few weather-related flight delays, I was especially anxious to retrieve my bags, hopeful but doubtful that they'd traveled on the same planes I had. As I waited, I watched. Clearly, my flight companions felt as I did. Noticeably relieved as they spotted their bags, several people appeared as though they might just hug their luggage upon retrieval. Someone commented that she felt naked without hers. Once I had mine in my hands, I wondered why I had worried so. Was my cargo all that precious, or was it merely weighing me down? I chuckled, contrasting this necessary baggage with the unnecessary, proverbial baggage to which I frequently refer when speaking of the kind we too often carry: continued guilt over our forgiven sins.

We understand grace, right? God's grace, by definition, is the unearned, undeserved favor and forgiveness of God in Christ. We've received His grace by faith. No longer condemned by the guilt of our sin, we're set free! So why do we claim our baggage of guilt and continue to carry it? Maybe we believe we still deserve the load, so we're quick to grab it when it comes into view. We recognize it as ours and—dare I say?—embrace it because of its familiarity. Maybe we feel exposed without it; we've struggled with this guilt for so long that it goes wherever we do. Sister in Christ, is this you? If you have it in your hands, it's unnecessarily weighing you down, because it's no longer yours. Storm-induced flight delays may be the reason we lose our physical luggage, but storms of sin cause us to claim the emotional baggage of guilt or condemnation.

DISCUSSION QUESTION 1 What does your favorite piece of luggage look like? What makes you like it so much? Compare it to your proverbial baggage. What do Romans 8:1–2 and Ephesians 2:4–5 say about condemnation and sin? As you read these verses and write your responses, envision laying this baggage at the foot of the cross, where Jesus took it from you, carried it for you, and suffered in your place so you could be free of all guilt and condemnation.

DISCUSSION QUESTION 2 Read and unpack the message of Romans 5:8. What does this verse tell you about the measure of God's love in action? What do you learn of His grace? Does He approach you only if you can step out of your own storm by your own doing?

Bask in God's redeeming love, which rescued you from sin through Christ's death on the cross and His victory at the empty tomb. He met you in your storm and saved you from it, as only He, the sinless Son of God, could do.

DISCUSSION QUESTION 3 Look up the following psalms. Then list God's actions for you:

Psalm 32:1

Psalm 34:22

Psalm 103:12

Which words resonate with you today? How will the Lord keep you from being condemned?

GO, AND SIN NO MORE

"Jesus said, 'Neither do I condemn you; go, and from now on sin no more' " (John 8:11). Jesus freed the woman caught in adultery and gave her direction for the new life she now possessed by faith. By His transforming power, she could willingly walk away from her former way of life and into the newness of life in her Redeemer.

You and I, by God's gracious gift of faith, are new creations in Christ (2 Corinthians 5:17). By the Holy Spirit's power, Christ lives in us (Colossians 1:27), enabling us to believe and to receive His power that even now is at work in us. Will we still struggle with sin? Will we face temptations of the flesh, the world, and the evil one? Yes, of course. But "He who is in [us] is greater than he who is in the world" (1 John 4:4). Jesus beckons us to turn from sin as we go in a new direction, following after Him. With His help, we can respond in faith and obedience to His compassionate grace and love.

DISCUSSION QUESTION 4 Equipped in Christ, how do we turn?

• Out of the darkness ➔ into _____ (1 Peter 2:9).

• Away from the _____ _____ ➔ to the _____ _____ (Colossians 3:9–10).

• Far from the former inability to understand _____ truth ➔ to the ability to discern it (1 Corinthians 2:12–14).

• Away from the attitude of "anything goes" ➔ to the recognition of _____ vs. _____ (1 John 2:21).

Greater than the ability to understand and recognize truth is the ability to live by it. We are no longer trapped and held hostage by our sin. We are free from the stranglehold it had upon us. In God's power and by His mercies (which are "new every morning," according to Lamentations 3:22–23), we are able to flee from sin's trappings and temptations and live in a manner "worthy of the Gospel" (Philippians 1:27). "His divine power has granted to us all things that pertain to life and godliness, through the knowledge of Him who called us to His own glory and excellence" (2 Peter 1:3).

One day, when Jesus returns, you and I will sin no more. Meanwhile, Jesus pursues a closer walk with us as He guides us in His Word. By His grace, we are growing, changing, and receiving renovation, day by day, because He is actively working in us.

GOD IS AT WORK

Sometimes I still wonder how God can possibly use my storms of sin for good. Have you wondered the same thing? Let's consider the riches of His grace for us in Christ. Let's remember that He may use these storms to turn our focus toward Him as we trust His redemption. He will help us see our need for our Savior. Perhaps there is a sin for which we need to repent, or perhaps we're clinging to something that we must release, fully surrendering it to Him. Nevertheless, He is working in us, and He wants to renovate us, transforming us into Christ's image.

DISCUSSION QUESTION 5 What do the following verses say of God's power and work in us? Circle God's action in each verse. Draw a line under *you, we,* or *us.* What is our role in God's power and work?

❖ "And I am sure of this, that He who began a good work in you will bring it to completion at the day of Jesus Christ" (Philippians 1:6).

❖ "It is God who works in you, both to will and to work for His good pleasure" (Philippians 2:13).

❖ "Now to Him who is able to do far more abundantly than all that we ask or think, according to the power at work within us, to Him be glory" (Ephesians 3:20–21).

> **R&R:** I pray He opens your eyes to see how He is working in your life right now, in His transformational, renovative way! How is He revealing Himself to you? How is He giving you purpose and a plan?

Stop whatever you're doing right now to rejoice that God is at work in your life, doing incomparably more than you can imagine. He who began His salvation work in you through His Word will carry it to its completion when Jesus returns. Meanwhile, He continues to work powerfully in and through you, enabling you to fulfill His purpose for His pleasure, all the way to the day of Christ. Rest and rejoice in these promises, whatever comes your way today, friends.

JOURNAL: What one takeaway today enables me to say, "I can be still because I know that He is God"?

DAY 5: RENOVATION

DISREPAIR

Out with the old and in with the new! Ah, the joys of home renovation. Sometimes it takes storm damage to prompt already-needed renovation to an older home. If our old appliances could talk, they'd say they've seen better days. Sometimes they function, and sometimes they don't. Cracks appear in the plaster walls. Foot-worn flooring needs to be replaced. But we've grown so accustomed to the disrepair, we often don't even notice. We joke that we will finally begin renovation if a storm furthers the deterioration, leaving us without a choice.

Joking aside, catastrophic storms can bring devastation to homes and lives, necessitating complete renovation and renewal. Countless people have suffered home damage from tornadoes, earthquakes, floods, fires, and other disasters. What a relief it is when their home is salvageable. Let the renovation begin.

> **R&R:** Has home renovation been a part of your life? Have you grown accustomed to a state of disrepair? Let this imagery rest before you as we continue.

Could we speak similarly to our sinful state? Have we grown so accustomed to our current condition that we fail to see the disrepair in our lives? Are we bringing dysfunction to a relationship? Are flaws apparent, within and without? Are we worn out from treading the same ground as we mess up again and again? Praise God that He found us to be worth salvaging! In Christ, we are redeemed, restored, and forgiven for our sins. The Lord may also use the storm of our sin and the damage it has done to have us recognize our need for renovation and to bring it about, with His help.

God began His renewing work in you when He chose you by His grace, through faith in your Baptism and through His Word. He continues that renovating, transformational work in you, renewing you day by day.

TRANSFORMATIONAL TRUTH

In our sin, it's all too easy to become caught up in the whirlwind of worldliness and conform to it. But God calls us to something different: "Do not be conformed to this world, but be transformed by the renewal of your mind, that by testing you may discern what is the will of God, what is good and acceptable and perfect" (Romans 12:2).

The refuge you have in Christ is unshakable, regardless of what's happening in the world. You don't have to fall into the trap of conformity Satan sets for you. Get into God's Word, where He reveals His perfect will. There, "You will know the truth, and the truth will set you free" (John 8:32). Jesus is the truth, the living Word! Only He can free you from the power of sin and Satan, and their threats against you.

The more you spend time in Scripture, the more you will think in terms of Scripture. The Word is renovating—restorative and transformational. It renews your heart and mind, providing a whole new way of living. As the Lord renovates your thoughts, He changes your priorities and your habits. "[You] are being transformed into the same image from one degree of glory to another. For this comes from the Lord who is the Spirit" (2 Corinthians 3:18).

DISCUSSION QUESTION 1 Review these verses: Romans 12:2; John 8:32; 2 Corinthians 3:18. What are the connecting points among them? How is the Lord working transformation in you?

Remember Psalm 46 as you live differently; you are being renovated daily, continually, into the image of Christ, by the Spirit's power within you. God is your strength and your refuge, especially as the going gets tough. You don't need to fear, even when Satan attacks, the world scoffs, or your flesh caves. God is the fortress that surrounds you and wards off every attack.

> **R&R:** Responding to God's grace and His power to transform, take a look at past changes you've made, at the renovation work that has already been done. Talk about it. How has He changed you, even within the past year? How does considering His previous work in you help you look ahead with anticipation?

BE KIND

God's renovative work through His Word, causing us to grow in the likeness of Christ, brings to mind several Christlike qualities I want to emulate. One in particular shows up in a popular catchphrase: *kindness*. It's a fruit of the Holy Spirit (see Galatians 5:22). The saying goes, "In a world where you can be anything, be kind." It sounds like Ephesians 4:32: "Be kind to one another, tenderhearted, forgiving one another, as God in Christ forgave you."

We need to hear this command, because our sin would have us be anything but kind. Our hearts are far from tender, and all too often they are hardened against those who have hurt us or others. Forgiveness may be the furthest thing from our minds.

I relate to the apostle Paul, who recorded his ongoing struggle with sin in Romans 7.

DISCUSSION QUESTION 2 Read Romans 7:19 (and the context, as time allows). What does Paul do that he does not want to do? What does he not do that he wants to do? This is my struggle too. How can you relate? Talk about it.

So where does that leave me? On my own, I'm incapable. Stuck. Unable. Maybe even unwilling. But I am not left on my own. I am forgiven, and I am being renovated. So are you!

DISCUSSION QUESTION 3 Return to Romans 7. Paul continues his discourse about his struggle with sin, right up to his climactic question in verse 24. Then, without a pause, Paul answers his own question at the beginning of verse 25. What does he ask? How does he answer his own question?

Read Ephesians 4:32 again, letting your eyes rest on the words "as God in Christ forgave you." God came to us, forgiving us even when we were unkind and hard-hearted. He traded our hearts of stone for hearts of flesh (Ezekiel 36:26) and filled us with faith, by the power of His Spirit. Praise Him!

Moreover, God doesn't merely put up with us. He loves us, delights in us, and continues His good work in us. "He who began a good work in you will bring it to completion at the day of Jesus Christ" (Philippians 1:6). His forgiving power rests upon us, even now. In response to Christ's saving, sacrificial love, and by His work in us, we can be kind, tenderhearted, and forgiving. We can, because the One who founded our faith (Hebrews 12:2) keeps and carries us in it too.

> **R&R:** Ask God for His strength and grace to enable you to forgive someone. Ask Him to help you show that same person kindness, approaching him or her with a tender heart and love, like Jesus does. Write this person's name and commit to carry out a plan, with God's help and by His grace.

As I confess my wayward thoughts and poor priorities to the Lord and repent of them, He forgives. He leads me, once again, to follow Jesus, seeking continual transformation that won't be complete until "the day of Jesus Christ" (Philippians 1:6), when He returns.

There's still merit to the phrase "In a world where you can be anything, be kind." But let us be reminded that we are forgiven. Reading the catchphrase in the light of the Gospel, and empowered by the One who has forgiven us, we can, by God's grace, be kind. In a world where people need Jesus more than anything, may they see Jesus in you and me!

In our storms of sin, Jesus does for us what He did for the woman caught in the act of adultery:

- ❖ He handles our accusers. They answer to Jesus, just as we do.

- ❖ He forgives us. Our mistakes and mess-ups are redeemed. We are freed from the guilt of an ill-spent past too.

- ❖ He makes renovation possible by the Holy Spirit's work. He empowers us to live a new life in His care and by His grace.

- ❖ He gives continual guidance through His perfect Word, in answer to prayer, and as He works through faithful people who speak truth into our lives.

> **R&R:** Which of the above is most difficult for you to believe that Jesus can (and does) do for you? Believe it; it's true! Pray about it.

> **R&R:** "God is our refuge and strength, a very present help in trouble" (Psalm 46:1). In light of all you've learned in this week's session, how does Jesus fulfill these words of the psalmist for you? What does your Refuge's *redemption* mean to you? What *renewal* do you receive? What *renovation* work does He do daily? What might your response be?

JOURNAL: What one takeaway today enables me to say, "I can be still because I know that He is God"?

VIEWER GUIDE

SESSION 2: THE STORM OF SIN

Turn to John 8:2–11.

"Lord" (John 8:11), from the Greek *kurios*: _____.

"Neither do I condemn you" (verse 11). Notice the personal assurance and certainty in Jesus' statement that served to demonstrate two things:

1. He did not come to _____ the world, but to _____ it (John 12:47).

2. He is God's Son, with the authority to _____ _____.

Trapped in a storm of sin, the adulterous woman expected condemnation, but received, instead, Christ's _____, and with it, _____—a brand new beginning!

Jesus refused to consider her _____ state to be her _____ condition.

In Jesus' mercy and grace, He sees beyond our current state, and He calls us to a permanent position: His _____ _____.

DISCUSS

> God is our refuge and strength, a very present help in trouble. Therefore we will not fear though the earth gives way, though the mountains be moved into the heart of the sea, though its waters roar and foam, though the mountains tremble at its swelling. . . . "Be still, and know that I am God." (Psalm 46:1–3, 10)

As you consider your sin, what do your roaring waters and trembling mountains look like? How is your storm brewing or blowing in a specific struggle with sin? What trouble has come because of this storm?

Can you see God working to calm you or calm the storm, helping you to trust Him in it? How do you know that He is God and R.E.S.T. (*refuge*, *ever*-present *strength* in *trouble*) in that truth? How or where do you see His help?

READY TO R.E.S.T.?

READ AND REFLECT: What do the Scriptures and this Bible study say about the storm of sin? What do they say about Jesus, your refuge in this storm? What were your biggest takeaways?

EXAMINE QUESTIONS AND EXPLORE ANSWERS: For greater understanding and for application, seek answers in Scripture and meditate upon the personal questions.

SHARE: Tell about your takeaways and your storm, with a group or alone, as you write or pray about them.

TRUST your Refuge, the One who provides *redemption* and *renewal*.

STORMS OF SICKNESS

THE BLEEDING WOMAN—MARK 5:25–34

DAY 1: WHEN IT ISN'T GETTING BETTER

MY SISTER'S STORM

Several years ago, my sister, Connie, and her family moved to our parents' farm in South Dakota. While her husband worked on the ranch, she began teaching in the nearby rural school. All was well, until suddenly Connie wasn't. She remembers, "My throat was continually sore, and I ran a low-grade fever. I felt run down all the time." She had struggled with off-and-on illness since childhood, so at first, she didn't make much of it. "But when I wasn't getting any better," she said, "I had to start doctoring." Following three visits to the clinic and a series of inconclusive hospital tests, Connie was referred to a medical center in Sioux Falls. Following that visit, she still had no diagnosis but was suffering. The next referral took her to the Mayo Clinic, where seven different doctors performed batteries of tests.

Connie continued:

> Mayo had never seen anything like it. They tested for a multitude of diseases to no avail. Not knowing was scary. Was it something I would die from? They finally "diagnosed" me with a virus (for which there weren't even tests) and told me, "You're just going to have to live with it." Meanwhile, I developed terrible pain behind my ears and in my hands and feet. I returned to Mayo for more tests and biopsies. They were concerned about cancer. I was concerned about many things. I felt awful. I had a new teaching job that I loved and two little boys, ages 2 and 4, but I couldn't give myself completely to my work or my family because of my constant pain."

The same year, Connie's older son was diagnosed with type 1 diabetes. As they were learning how to deal with his disease, he was concerned about his mama; he didn't want to leave her side. It was heartbreaking when he asked if she was going to die.

Mayo referred Connie to a specialist, who provided treatments to help ease the pain, which at least enabled her to get through each day. Faced with the possibility that she would never recover, she attempted to treat the symptoms and learn to live with them. "I was scared I would never feel like the old me again. For two and a half years, I lived this way, resigned to the fact that this was my new normal."[27]

A WOMAN'S STORM OF SICKNESS—BASED ON MARK 5:25–34 (SEE ALSO MATTHEW 9:20–22; LUKE 8:43–48)

Pain was her constant companion, and her only companion for some time. Sickness and isolation defined her days. Bleeding was normal for her and definitely nothing new. Maybe these storms were what drew her into the crowd and to the Teacher, as people were calling Him. She knew the risk was great. Would someone recognize her and shout, "Unclean!"? Desperation led her to go anyway—desperation and hope.

For twelve years, she'd sunk under the wild waves of her personal storm. Uncontrolled bleeding had made her unclean. In addition to her suffering, she was shunned by her community and cast away from her family. According to the law, if she were even to touch another person, she would defile that person and could be charged with a crime. Even the chair she sat on and the pallet that was her bed were unclean. She had tried everything, every known cure. The doctors had no solution, though she had spent all her money on treatments. Every option was gone. And still the bleeding continued.

Then she heard about Jesus. He was healing the sick. He was performing miracles. A miracle is what she needed.

She believed that this Healer, this Miracle Worker, could make her well again, so she took the risk. She made her way into the crowd. There were so many people pushing and straining toward Jesus, pressing against Him. Some called out, "Master!" Others cried, "Teacher, heal me!" So many people in pain. "Could they be as desperate as I?" she thought. She squeezed past the others to approach Him. She bent low and hid her face, hoping she wouldn't be seen.

She knew that if she could just touch Him, if she could reach far enough to feel the hem of His robe—even just the fringe—she would be healed. She reached out, and something incredible happened. Just as her fingers touched the edge of His robe, her body felt immediately different. Miraculously, the bleeding stopped. She was healed!

Although the crowds still pressed around Him on every side, Jesus abruptly stopped and stood still. He turned. "Who touched My garments?" He asked (Mark 5:30). His followers shook their heads in confusion, stating what appeared to be obvious: "You see the crowd pressing around You" (verse 31).

The woman was terrified. If she admitted what she had done, she could become the center of condemnation. Everyone knew she was unclean. With her in their midst, they could all be unclean too. Not only that, by her touch, she had defiled the Teacher. But it was obvious that He knew she was the one who had touched His robe. She could no longer hide.

Trembling, she approached Jesus and fell at His feet. Everyone in the crowd stared as she spoke. She told Jesus the whole truth—why she had touched Him and how she was healed instantly. Jesus looked on her with compassionate love. "Daughter, your faith has made you well; go in peace, and be healed of your disease" (verse 34).

Hearing these tender words, the woman knew she had received healing, in body and soul, by Jesus' power. His grace covered her and made her whole; she was forgiven and clean! Even more, He had called her daughter, a beloved child of God and an heir to His kingdom. His words proclaimed to her—and to everyone who heard—that her sickness and her sin were taken away, replaced by His healing and mercy. (Portions of this narrative were published in *Stepping Out*.[28])

> **R&R:** Pause to ponder the story of this woman's storm. Read Mark 5:25–34, then write what stood out to you. What was the immediate takeaway?

DISCUSSION QUESTION 1 "God is our refuge and strength, a very present help in trouble" (Psalm 46:1). In what ways did Jesus fulfill these words for this woman? How was He her refuge in her storm of sickness?

The bleeding woman reached for physical healing but received, instead, a remedy for body and soul. She also received relationship in the family of God, for Jesus called her "daughter."

DISCUSSION QUESTION 2 "Be still, and know that I am God. I will be exalted among the nations, I will be exalted in the earth" (Psalm 46:10). Picture this woman's life following her encounter with Christ. Perhaps she knew these words of the psalmist. How do you think they would have spoken to her? How was Jesus exalted in her life already? How could He be exalted through her witness to the world?

PRAYER IN MY SISTER'S STORM

My sister, herself a prayer warrior, became the recipient of countless prayers throughout her ordeal. It pained her that she lacked the physical and mental energy to pray for others as she had previously done:

I've always prayed so much for other people, and I wanted so badly to pray more during this difficult time. Instead, I could only manage, "Please help me to get better." I knew God understood. And I never blamed God for the illness. I may have questioned why, but I didn't doubt God or turn away from Him.

After two and a half years of suffering, Connie began to heal and eventually returned to her old self. Today, Connie exclaims, "I thank God that He restored me to good health!" While she is rarely sick now, she fights fear whenever the pain returns, but so far, it has never come to stay.

My sister suffered much not because of the physicians, as the bleeding woman had (Mark 5:26), but throughout her medical care because they had no solutions and offered little relief. In faith, she reached out to God. She knew His peace and trusted His sovereignty, even when she thought she might never be healed of her mysterious illness.

With strong faith, Connie continues to come to Jesus in prayer. She knows how to be still; she knows that He is her God, her Healer and Comforter. He is mightier than her storm, and He is exalted in her life!

> **R&R:** What storms of sickness have you endured? Maybe you have struggled with a series of unrelated health issues; maybe you've battled a chronic illness or faced a recent diagnosis. Perhaps the storm has passed, maybe you're still in it, or maybe it's yet to come. Share.

Know that you are not alone in your storm; He is with you. Be still, and know that He is God, incomparably more powerful than your storm—your struggle with any sickness.

JOURNAL: What one takeaway today enables me to say, "I can be still because I know that He is God"?

DAY 2: HIS HEALING TOUCH

WHAT'S WRONG?

When a storm of sickness blows your way, how do you initially react? When you're not well, you want to get to the bottom of it, right? It's unsettling when you can't define the storm that's raging inside of you.

I was blindsided by a sudden storm following the birth of my twins. For months, an undiagnosed illness had taken me down for the count. Once I had a diagnosis (Grave's disease), I knew what I was facing and how to proceed. Thanks to God's work through my physicians, medicine, and prayer, healing did come. My thyroid disease is monitored and managed. Praise the Lord!

What was wrong with the bleeding woman, beyond the obvious? Have you wondered what type of blood loss she endured? In Matthew's account of her story, the Greek word *haimorroeo* means "hemorrhage," which refers specifically to menstrual blood flow (see Leviticus 15:33).[29]

The woman's debilitating condition was likely menorrhagia,[30] and while it's treatable today, there was no help in her day. She lived with continual menstrual bleeding for twelve long years. Doctors may have used combinations of natural substances such as oil, wine, herbs, and other plants as treatment. They may have offered superstitious remedies, some with exotic, expensive ingredients for potions, promising a cure. "Some of their practices actually increased their patients' suffering."[31] "The [Jewish] Talmud lists eleven cures for such ailments, all of which we would consider superstitious."[32] One example was an instruction to place the afflicted person at a fork in the road with a cup of wine in her hand, then frighten her from behind, saying, "Arise from thy flux!"[33] Based on archaeological discoveries of knives, saws, tweezers, forceps, chisels, and scoops dating to 1500 BC and beyond, historians believe that some physicians may have practiced surgery as well.[34]

Consider the combined impact of the woman's physical symptoms, financial devastation, and societal segregation. She would have suffered physically from anemia, fatigue, and faintness. She would have been financially destitute at the doctors' failed attempts to provide healing. Mosaic Law stated that her condition made her unclean (Leviticus 15:25–26). The Law also warned that the touch of an unclean person contaminated those in contact (Leviticus 5:3), mandating a ritual cleansing (Leviticus 15:21). This pale, weak woman was perpetually unclean and was likely separated by law from her family. Imagine the lack of human touch for twelve years, with the exception, perhaps, of the physicians' touch, which brought only more pain. If she was married, sexual relations with her husband would have been out of the question, and this sickness could have even served as grounds for her husband to divorce her (Deuteronomy 24:1). Adding insult to injury, in her unclean state, she was even forbidden to worship at the synagogue (Leviticus 15:29–31).

> **R&R:** Choose at least one of the Mosaic Law references and examine it to understand how the law read. Which of these restrictions would have been most difficult for you, if you were this woman?

THE SLIGHTEST TOUCH

While this woman wanted to go unnoticed, she believed Jesus' healing could be communicated through even the slightest touch, so she timidly approached Him from behind. She was understandably afraid to be seen, knowing that her unclean state forbade her to be present, let alone within touching distance of others.[35]

DISCUSSION QUESTION 1 Why is it especially significant that this healing involved touch (since Jesus sometimes healed with only a word)? Was it her physical touch that provided healing?

DISCUSSION QUESTION 2 Jesus healed countless people—the crippled, leprous, blind, mute, fevered, demon-possessed, and more. What do you read in Luke 6:19 that may have impacted the woman's brave decision to approach Jesus and touch Him?

Many were touching Jesus, clamoring to come near the Teacher, the Healer. They were pressing in on all sides. He was surrounded, fairly crushed, by the crowd. After Jesus' sudden halt, the crowd would have bumped and pressed all the more. It's no wonder that the disciples marveled at Jesus' question, "Who touched My garments?" (Mark 5:30).

DISCUSSION QUESTION 3 At the moment of the woman's touch, three things happened. What were they?

Simultaneously, as strength surged through the woman's body, Jesus felt power go out from Him. The power that went out from Jesus is the same power of the Spirit (Luke 4:14), the power of the Lord to heal (Luke 5:17) that He possessed. Notice that power went out *from* Him, not *of* Him. It is not a power that can be depleted![36]

Jesus didn't perform this miracle involuntarily, either. Because He is God, He knew of her plan and allowed Himself the proximity and opportunity to be within her reach. He knew she would—at the same instant of her touch—receive healing.[37]

The woman's faith in Jesus' healing made her well. It was likely a simple faith. She simply believed in Jesus. She dared to touch. She didn't utter a word. How incredible is His knowledge, His compassion, and His power to answer an unspoken cry! She was touched by the mercy of God, even as she touched the hem of His garment. "When you are hanging on by a thread, may it be the hem of His garment" (author unknown).

> **R&R:** I find tremendous comfort in knowing that when I'm barely hanging on, I can reach out for Jesus, who has hold of me already. The thread of His hem is all the touch I need. When have you found yourself hanging on by a thread? Share your thoughts.

Why doesn't healing happen every time people of faith reach out for it? We know God is good, so why isn't there always relief from our pain or removal of our anxiety when we ask? God will act out of love, to be sure. However, our desire for Him to move in a certain direction and according to our timetable does not mean that He will. "For My thoughts are not your thoughts, neither are your ways My ways, declares the LORD. For as the heavens are higher than the earth, so are My ways higher than your ways and My thoughts than your thoughts" (Isaiah 55:8–9). Trust that He will move in perfect alignment with His purpose, in His higher ways, His wisdom, and His will. What does it mean to trust in Him?

- Believe in the One whose promises are always perfectly kept.

- Remember His past promises already fulfilled.

- Rely on His faithfulness and not on the present outlook.

- "Wait for the LORD; be strong, and let your heart take courage; wait for the LORD!" (Psalm 27:14).

- Know that He is your refuge and strength, your present help in today's trouble.

> **R&R:** Circle the reminders that you find most helpful while you wait for healing and as you persevere. Maybe you have others. Share them here:

The Lord comes through for you. He acts on your behalf, and as He does, He reveals His glory to the world. Because of His victory over sickness and pain, disease and death, you can wait on Him in confidence and certain hope for final and eternal healing.

SINGLED OUT IN A CROWD

Consider the woman's "fear and trembling" (Mark 5:33) immediately following the tremendous transmission of power that provided her healing. Jesus singled her out. She would have rightly feared rebuke from the One she had touched; according to the Law, her touch was contaminating. As everyone would see, however, He singled her out not only for her good but also for the watching world and for His glory. Jesus wasn't going to let the now-healed woman retreat into the crowd without publicly commending her faith and announcing to all that she was fully healed. As "a testimony to the crowd, Jesus insisted that the miracle be made known."[38] It may have seemed that the attention would only lead to her community ostracizing her even more, but Jesus turned the tables entirely. He who could not be contaminated removed her contamination! "Jesus' authority trump[s] any ritual contamination."[39]

DISCUSSION QUESTION 4 Imagine yourself in the woman's place. After your daring touch and instantaneous healing, how would you have reacted to Jesus' question, "Who touched Me?" followed by His knowing gaze upon you?

Why did Jesus have the woman publicly explain herself? Author and educator Jane Fryar notes, "Jesus wanted her to know that He did not begrudge her healing. He wanted her to leave with His peace (Mark 5:34), not in shame or fear. And He wanted the crowds to see He did not despise the weak."[40] The late author Marlys Taege Moberg noted, "This wasn't an accusation; it was an invitation for the woman to come forward. Jesus would use her touch to teach."[41] When He searched the crowd, He was not wondering who or where. He knew, even as He waited for the woman to come forward, encouraging her with His gentle words. He asked for the sake of everyone present. His question commanded an answer and powerfully revealed truth to the crowd.

She spilled the whole story: her condition and her suffering; her need, which she knew He could fulfill; the miracle when she touched Him. Luke's account recalls that she "declared in the presence of all the people why she had touched Him, and how she had been immediately healed" (Luke 8:47). Imagine her rush of words, chronicling twelve years of suffering during this brief interaction—suffering that ended abruptly the moment she was healed.

JOURNAL: What one takeaway today enables me to say, "I can be still because I know that He is God"?

DAY 3: DAUGHTER

"YOUR FAITH HAS MADE YOU WELL"

Envision a clamoring crowd witnessing this exchange: a daring touch, a miraculous healing, an invitation for explanation. And then, an announcement: "Your faith has made you well" (Mark 5:34). It sounds like a climactic scene from a movie, but this brief scene is a tiny slice right out of history.

Jesus' pronouncement to the community of the bleeding woman's cleansing meant no more isolation, no more storm of stigma. A ritualistic purification service would not be necessary; she was declared clean! No longer an outcast, she was restored. Her refuge, Jesus, provided remedy for both body and soul. Her healing was complete.

DISCUSSION QUESTION 1 What else would the woman be able to resume, now that she was healed and pronounced clean?

DISCUSSION QUESTION 2 Based on what we learned about physicians and their many mystical treatments, what was one important reason why Jesus clarified how the woman was healed?

All who witnessed Jesus' healing work heard Him say it was the woman's faith that made her well. It was not some magical touch or mystical power conferred by Jesus' garment. It was a miracle of Christ. By His words to her, Jesus removed any possibility of superstition that could have been held by the woman or anyone in the crowd.

Pause to consider how Jesus' announcement to this woman applies to you and me. "Your faith has made you well" (verse 34). By His perfect life and sacrificial death, Jesus fulfilled the old covenant, which included every ritualistic ceremonial cleansing required under the laws of Moses. Jesus' blood, shed for us, rescued us from the sickness of sin and death. By faith alone we receive the forgiveness of our sin without need of any ritual purification service on our part. With repentant hearts, we confess and—praise the Lord—we are clean!

Oh, the beautiful truth in this healing account! We are saved through the blood of Christ, shed in our place, though His suffering was incomparably greater. But "with His wound we are healed" (Isaiah 53:5). By faith in His redemptive work, we are made well.

DISCUSSION QUESTION 3 Don't miss the greater purpose for this and every miracle Jesus performed. In healing this woman, Jesus revealed that He is God. He is the fulfillment of every messianic prophesy. What does 2 Corinthians 1:20 say regarding every one of God's promises?

Jesus is the remedy for every sickness and sin. God's work in Christ centers on the fullness of healing—the restoration—of all sinners, of all creation.

DAUGHTER

During my freshman year of high school, I had my own credit account at our local grocery store. Well, okay, it was my parents' account, put in place for my sister Connie and me to use. Our farm was very rural, so we girls rented an apartment in town that was closer to school. My sister, a senior, could commandeer our meals and grocery trips, but we were both given access to the credit available. We needed only to tell the clerk, "Put that on Dick Hudson's account," and it was done. No credit card was needed; no cash was exchanged. It was just a manual ledger for special customers.

The identity of being his daughter meant something. Dad was widely respected and trusted across his rural community. When someone read my name, they'd say with a smile, "Oh, you're Dick Hudson's daughter." I needed the credit my parents provided. I depended on their guidance, and I trusted they would always take care of me. I was their dependent child, growing under their grace, and I hoped I was starting to resemble them.

As much as my parents were trustworthy, God is entirely and eternally dependable. The identity of being God's daughter means everything. He gives perfect guidance by His Word and through the work of the Spirit. All the credit goes to my Father—the One who made me His own in Christ. When someone sees me, I hope they will say, "Oh, you're God's daughter," and they'll smile, because—by His grace—I'm starting to resemble Him!

R&R: Have you been identified by your name, your appearance, or your association with someone? You are someone's daughter, sister, aunt, mother, colleague, or friend. Think of a time when you were pleased to be identified by your association with someone. Write about it and share.

R&R: You are God's daughter! Ponder the reasons someone might recognize you as His child. How are you growing to resemble Him more every day?

A NEW IDENTITY

Jesus provided far more than physical healing to the bleeding woman. He gave her a new identity: daughter, "a tender address used nowhere else in Jesus' recorded words."[42] She was adopted by the Lord Himself. By faith, she received a place in God's family, and that meant everything!

Her own family may have abandoned her, but the Refuge in her storm afforded her an abundance. He called her into relationship with Himself when He called her "daughter." He turned on her His undivided attention. He provided her individual care and healing, He commended her faith, and He supplied the remedy for her sickness and sin.

Jesus revealed His unique concern for a *daughter* in the family of God, for a storm specific only to a woman. A man could not receive this kind of healing. Do you know that Jesus provides the same individual care and concern for you? Don't hesitate or fear, but confidently reach out for healing and forgiveness to the One who calls you daughter. He is with you in your adversity, responds with His loving touch, and reminds you of your true identity.

DISCUSSION QUESTION 4 How do the following verses speak together to your familial relationship with the Lord? What words stand out to you most? Read Romans 8:15; Galatians 4:4–7; Ephesians 1:4–6.

Adopted. Let the meaning of that word sink in. Consider the cost to a family today that adopts a child. Then consider the incomparably greater cost to God that was necessary to bring you into His family. He paid the ransom to redeem you from your slavery to sin, and His payment came at the cross of Christ. His life was given in exchange for yours so you would be set free to become a member of His family. He has made you His child.

THE PERFECT PARENT

A mother knows. Well, most of the time. Typically, when my children were sick, I could determine if a trip to the doctor was in order. I could test for a fever by pressing my lips to their foreheads; I could diagnose minor maladies with ease. But there were times I overreacted, running to urgent care unnecessarily. Other times, I downplayed symptoms when something more serious was going on in their little bodies.

> **R&R:** Is self-diagnosis a strength of yours? When have you hit or missed the mark when you or a loved one was sick?

I am far from a perfect parent, but I will do anything to assist my children when they are sick or struggling. When they're emotionally or physically hurt, I hurt with them. If it were possible, I would take their illnesses upon myself, if it meant they would receive relief. Now that they are young adults, my children call when they're ill, knowing they will receive help, empathy, and prayer. That is how deeply I care. With this in mind, think about your own care for your child, niece or nephew, grandchild, or another loved one for whom you would do anything. Then consider your Lord, who is the perfect parent. He knows your loved one's pain infinitely more than you do. The depth of His care is incomparable to that of anyone else.

Jesus knows your pain. He felt your affliction and shouldered your sicknesses in His own suffering throughout His Passion and on the cross:

Blood and sweat dripped from His brow.

Whips broke the flesh of His back.

Thorns of the crown cut into His skull.

The crossbeam's weight bore down on Him as He carried it toward Calvary's hill.

Nails cut holes into His hands and feet.

Pain ripped through His body as He hung on the cross.

He took your pain upon Himself. When you hurt, He hurts with you. He knows your pain.

DISCUSSION QUESTION 5 He is the perfect parent. He wants you to approach Him confidently to "receive mercy and find grace to help in time of need" (Hebrews 4:16). If we reach out and "touch even His garments" (Mark 5:28), He does not turn us away. Read the following passages and combine what you find to write a description of your heavenly Father, who He is and what He does for you, His daughter.

- 1 John 3:1–2

- Romans 8:38–39

- Philippians 4:19

- Colossians 1:12–14

- Hebrews 12:5–6

We trust that we are who God says we are: loved and forgiven daughters of God, chosen in Christ! He endured the agony of the cross and died in our place. He conquered the grave and provides for us an eternal home in heaven.

JOURNAL: What one takeaway today enables me to say, "I can be still because I know that He is God"?

DAY 4: TRUST AND PEACE IN THE STORM

DIFFICULT TO DEFINE

Sometimes sicknesses are difficult to define. In this information age, an online search may offer an answer, but more likely it adds to our concern when we see the scope of possibilities that our malady may be. Perhaps the difficulty in defining your sickness lies in the nature of your symptoms. You might say that days are dreary, anxious, or worrisome, and you feel a general malaise. Maybe, like me, you struggle with one or more forms of anxiety (situational, generalized, or social anxiety, among others).[43]

Consider how the crowd between Jesus and the bleeding woman was a barrier, an obstacle in the way of the woman approaching Jesus. Think about the metaphorical barrier keeping you from approaching Jesus when your sickness looks like one or more of the following:

- You're embarrassed that you feel this way, so you think you should tough it out on your own. After all, you tell yourself, others have greater concerns.

- You rely on self-help advice because the culture keeps saying, "You've got this."

- You believe you are undeserving of help or healing, so you don't ask for it.

- You decide you are incapable of receiving a cure, so you quit seeking one.

As with any illness, the symptoms of anxiety, depression, and related mental and emotional struggles are varied, and they are real. While my intent is not to play doctor, I will tell you this: mental maladies are every bit as physical as others.[44] Just as you seek the Lord's help and wisdom for other illnesses, I encourage you to take any mental and emotional struggles straight to the Great Physician as well.

- You were never called to tough it out on your own. Your concerns, great and small, matter to the Lord and to those who love you.

- While the culture says, "You've got this," you and I both know better. God's got this—and us—in His grip.

- Because of sin, we are undeserving of every good thing, but that's where grace enters in. God freely gives us every good gift by His grace: undeserved, unearned favor for us in Christ!

- Trust Him to work in you; nothing is impossible for God. He may help or heal you through a trusted friend, a Christian counselor or life coach, or a pastor. He may work through an excellent practitioner or therapist who can accurately prescribe a helpful regimen, a diet plan, or a medication.

> **R&R:** Can you relate with any of the metaphorical barriers mentioned above? Circle those that speak to you, and connect them to the corresponding words of encouragement (also above).

Maybe this storm of sickness continues to blow. Answers aren't obvious, and healing hasn't come. And yet, in the midst of it, you receive some semblance of peace. In *Hope When Your Heart Breaks,* Pastor Michael Newman puts it this way:

> When the turbulence of . . . struggle[s] swirl and rage in your heart and soul, Jesus calms the storm. Everything may still be unsettled. Solutions and resolution may still elude you. But somehow, in some mysterious way, Jesus . . . fills you with peace. It's not self-help; it's God's help.[45]

Trust that God is helping you. Even when you have not received the physical healing you seek, hear Him say, "Daughter!" and receive His peace.

DISCUSSION QUESTION 1 Can you relate to the words from Pastor Newman? Whether they do or don't speak to your situation now, does it help to know that peace is possible in the midst of struggle? When have you received unexpected peace, even if some things were unsettled and solutions eluded you?

Pastor Newman also shared these comforting words of truth:

> When you're down and out, God does not get disgusted. When you are helpless and immobilized, God does not become impatient with you. In your lowest moments of weakness, God doesn't grit His teeth and tolerate you as a bothersome inconvenience. When you are needy, God doesn't complain about your lack of toughness or grumble that you are taking too much of His time. His heart goes out to you. Compassion wells up within Him. Kindness and concern collect in the depths of His being and spill out in tender and restoring action. God's Word describes His demeanor toward fragile followers like us: "As a father shows compassion to his children, so the LORD shows compassion to those who fear Him" (Psalm 103:13).[46]

DISCUSSION QUESTION 2 You are the child of your heavenly Father, and He extends His compassion to you. Discover more about the Lord's compassion in these passages: Matthew 9:35–38; 14:14–21; Luke 7:11–15. Look for the word *compassion* in each account. In what ways did Jesus reveal His compassion and extend it out of love for His people? Note another interaction with a woman and Jesus' individual care for her. Do you believe He extends His compassion to you too?

YOUR WORTH

Are there storms related to sickness that have caused you to question your value? When you wonder about your worth, think on this: an item's value is determined by the amount someone is willing to spend to acquire it. Your value—your worth—is determined by God's payment for you: the life of His Son. Your value is proven in God's payment. Period. Nothing you do changes your worth to your Father. You are no less valuable when you are weak, ill, struggling, or suffering.

DISCUSSION QUESTION 3 Knowing this, what words describe your value, your worth? What does that mean regarding your identity?

When I'm reminded of my worth and identity as the Lord's child, sometimes I envision climbing onto Jesus' lap like a child. I picture myself like one of the children He took into His arms and blessed, just after He said, "Let the children come to Me; do not hinder them, for to such belongs the kingdom of God. Truly, I say to you, whoever does not receive the kingdom of God like a child shall not enter it" (Mark 10:14–15). My daughter, Courtney, remarked about these verses:

> Children are fully dependent; they know they can't do things on their own. They trust that their parents are going to take care of them. In the same way, we should have that faith, reliance, and dependence on God. We need Him like a child needs her parents. Oftentimes, when we talk about a childlike faith, we think of it as being a blind faith, but that's not what it means. It's important for us to have an informed faith and know why we believe what we believe; yet at the same time, we're called to be like children with a trusting dependence on God, our Father. . . . He welcomes us with open arms, just like He did the little children.[47]

DISCUSSION QUESTION 4 List the ways you are dependent upon your heavenly Father. Do you trust Him for your every need? Where would you like to grow in that trust?

THE GREAT EXCHANGE

The bleeding woman sought Jesus' help and reached out her hand. As He took her sickness, she was filled with His healing power. Even more profoundly, He took her sin, and she was filled with His grace! Recently, I found myself comparing this great exchange to another. When God asks us to give our anxiety to Him, He trades it for His peace. "Do not be anxious about anything, but in everything by prayer and supplication with thanksgiving let your requests be made known to God. And the peace of God, which surpasses all understanding, will guard your hearts and your minds in Christ Jesus" (Philippians 4:6–7). He makes the trade, yet retains every bit of His grace, power, and peace!

The image of the trade took me back to an anxious moment at a women's retreat. During a break, I walked around the grounds and wandered to the end of a boat dock in the lake at the center. I was anxious about many things as I stood there, praying. When I looked up, I thought of fishermen: the one who stands at the end of the dock, casting his line into the lake, and the one in his boat beyond the dock, casting his net across the water.

Cast: to throw something forcefully in a specified direction. Or, in my version, to let go with gusto! "[Cast] all your anxieties on Him, because He cares for you" (1 Peter 5:7). I threw out an invisible line, casting it on the Lord as I talked to Him. He knows when I'm struggling with anxious thoughts. Not only does He want me to bring them to Him in prayer, but He also wants me to cast my anxiety upon Him. More than merely laying my issues at His feet, I launched them toward the Lord. I prayed that I may let go with gusto, knowing that God would take them into His capable hands. He reeled in for me peace in their place.

> **R&R:** Take every anxious thought to the One who already knows it; cast it on the One who cares more than anyone else. Let go with gusto. Even if you don't immediately feel the exchange, trust that God is at work. He is making the trade and reeling in His peace, just for you, guarding both your heart and your mind in your Savior, Jesus. Write about it.

BUT WHAT IF?

Trust God's persistent work in you, even when you've failed to let go and have reeled in your anxiety and worry yet again. He also works through others, who will give you a good word and remind you that you're not alone with your worries and what-ifs. Remember, He trades your anxiety for His peace.

My friend Karen Sue penned this piece during the early weeks of the COVID-19 pandemic. God gave her a good word to share, and it was just the reminder I needed:

> Let me just tell you, I can worry with the best of 'em. And COVID-19 has added so many new opportunities to worry. Where will I buy [my favorite] peanut butter? . . . Where will I buy toilet paper? Will Rocky Mountain Chocolate Factory survive this economic downturn? . . . Will I get COVID-19? Or my loved ones? Will we die? . . .
>
> Ironically, COVID-19 has forced me to change. Especially with my husband being in health care, and with all the front line news and research he is reading to stay current . . ., we are understandably overwhelmed. Early on I realized the "what ifs" were going to just crush me. I have to constantly remind myself of what Jesus commanded in [Matthew 6:34], "Do not worry about tomorrow" [NIV]. When I start to worry, I have to "STOP" and think about *today*. Live today. . . .
>
> Jesus totally lived His life on earth "not worrying about tomorrow." His life was all about "live today." . . . Jesus lived the calling of this moment whether it was healing the sick, calming the storm, or teaching His disciples. . . .
>
> As Jesus Christ warned, we will have tribulation. Currently that tribulation is COVID-19. But Jesus also promised that He would overcome the world [John 16:33]. . . . Do not worry about tomorrow. **Live today!**[48]

> **R&R:** What kind of what-ifs about tomorrow lead you to worry today? What reminders can you place before you to focus on today? What is God calling you to do this day?

JOURNAL: What one takeaway today enables me to say, "I can be still because I know that He is God"?

DAY 5: REMEDIES

HOME REMEDIES

From the practical to the peculiar, home remedies are common. If you've received chicken noodle soup to treat a cold, honey-lemon tea to soothe a sore throat, or lemon-lime soda to ease an upset stomach (my dad's personal favorite), you know what I mean. Sometimes a home remedy is just the trick to treat a symptom, and many of them are beneficial. But some are superstitions, misleading, or potentially harmful, as we learned about the treatments of the era when we studied the woman with the flow of blood.

> **R&R:** Name your favorite home remedies and why they're just the trick for certain symptoms. Are you aware of any superstitious remedies or the kind that could cause harm? Share.

What can we say of home remedies for our common sickness of sin? We can try all kinds of remedies, but all are as futile as this woman's treatments at the hands of doctors of her day: she "was no better but rather grew worse" (Mark 5:26). Our attempts to self-medicate our sin are no more effective than slapping a bandage on internal bleeding. Yes, the woman's unmet physical needs led her to Jesus. But as we've learned, her real needs were much greater. Certainly, she was seeking refuge and relief from the storm raging in her body and impacting every aspect of her life. But Jesus' healing saved her from a suffering far worse.

Healed used here actually means "saved" in Greek. In Jesus, she received a blessed combination (verse 34): physical healing ("be healed of your disease") and spiritual healing ("go in peace").[49] This is the peace of God, "which surpasses all understanding" (Philippians 4:7). Far greater than bodily wellness is the unparalleled well-being that comes from salvation. God's miraculous work in giving His peace is beyond the limitations of our human reasoning or intellect. We receive it by faith. Jesus said, "Peace I leave with you; My peace I give to you. Not as the world gives do I give to you. Let not your hearts be troubled, neither let them be afraid" (John 14:27).

DISCUSSION QUESTION 1 When you pray for help and healing, do you limit the scope of your request? If so, what limits do you place on it? Why do you think that is?

Jesus' healing saved this woman from eternal sickness and eternal death. He restored her to eternal life! He provided a free and full faith relationship with Him. Jesus' remedy made her whole in every way.

THE GREAT PHYSICIAN

Maybe your struggle with sickness continues. Maybe it has not yet come, but you fear that something will, in time. My sweet sister in Christ, do not despair. Continue to take it to the Lord in prayer. Know this: He is with you in it. He hears. He knows. He is the Great Physician. Seek His wisdom and ask for trust, even as He may bring you healing through the help of a doctor or therapist, and as He continues to work through the prayers of faith-filled people who are holding you up in your struggle. Trust that He has already given you His healing touch. He heals you by the power of the Holy Spirit, who lives and abides in you as a guarantee of your future inheritance in heaven. "In Him you also, when you heard the word of truth, the gospel of your salvation, and believed in Him, were sealed with the promised Holy Spirit, who is the guarantee of our inheritance until we acquire possession of it, to the praise of His glory" (Ephesians 1:13–14).

Trust in Jesus' healing forgiveness that truly makes you whole. He "is able to do far more abundantly than all that [you] ask or think, according to the power at work within [you]" (Ephesians 3:20). In light of the narrative of the bleeding woman, look at His remedy like this:

- No longer dead in your sin, you are made alive in Christ.

- No longer contaminated by sin, you are clean.

- No longer a slave, you are His child, an heir with Christ, and an heir of heaven.

- No longer an outcast, you are restored.

DISCUSSION QUESTION 2 Read Psalm 59:16. When have you faced a day of distress? How was God "a fortress and a refuge" in it? Did you know it at the time? Create a prayer from this psalm, regarding one particular storm of sickness (past or present).

Maybe you can relate to the chronic nature of the bleeding woman's illness. Maybe you wonder if you will ever be well. Though you may have never been cast out or called unclean, you still know the pain of isolation that comes when you're ill. In what storm of sickness have you longed for the healing touch of Jesus?

❖ Reach out your hand in confident hope to the One who created you. He calls you His workmanship, His masterpiece (Ephesians 2:10). He knit you together in your mother's womb (Psalm 139:13). He formed and knows the work of every cell in your body. He knows the storm of your pain, and He hears your every prayer.

❖ Fall at the feet of the One who would stop and be still just for you. He fills you with His perfect peace.

❖ Hear the tender words of the One who calls you daughter and looks on you with compassionate love.

The bleeding woman, in her storm of sickness, sought physical healing in a desperate attempt for help. Jesus gave her what she sought, and so much more! She found refuge in relationship with the Savior who called her daughter. She received relief from her disease and release from the laws that held her captive. She could be still and know that He is *her* God, her very present help in her storm.

This side of eternity, we may not know the purpose for our pain, but we can take heart that Jesus, our Redeemer, provides us with the ultimate healing. "Daughter, your faith has made you well" (Mark 5:34). He gives us help and hope in our storms of sickness too. Take refuge in the One who provides a perfect remedy for all that ails you! Be still and know.

R&R: "God is our refuge and strength, a very present help in trouble" (Psalm 46:1). In light of all you have learned in this week's session, in what ways does Jesus fulfill these words of the psalmist for you? What does His gift of *relationship* mean to you? Remember, He calls you daughter! What is the *remedy* to your sickness of sin that He provides daily and eternally? What might your response be?

JOURNAL: What one takeaway today enables me to say, "I can be still because I know that He is God"?

VIEWER GUIDE

SESSION 3: STORMS OF SICKNESS

_____ _____ to Jesus.

Turn to Mark 5:24–34.

Jesus persistently sought out the healed woman. He was even more determined to address her than she was to avoid detection! He sought her out

• to honor her _____;

• to pronounce her _____, for all to hear; and

• to speak into her life with words of _____ and _____.

"Daughter" (Mark 5:34), from the Greek *thugatér*: _____.

In her storm of sickness, the bleeding woman reached for physical healing, but received, instead, a _____ to all that ailed her (physically and spiritually) as well as _____ in the family of God. She could be still and know that He is God, her Father and Savior.

"Jesus loves me! . . . Little ones to Him belong; They are _____, but He is _____" (*LSB* 588:1).

"My grace is sufficient for you, for My power is made perfect in weakness" (2 Corinthians 12:9).

DISCUSS

> God is our refuge and strength, a very present help in trouble. Therefore we will not fear though the earth gives way, though the mountains be moved into the heart of the sea, though its waters roar and foam, though the mountains tremble at its swelling. . . . "Be still, and know that I am God." (Psalm 46:1–3, 10)

As you consider your storms of sickness, what do your roaring waters and trembling mountains look like? How is your storm brewing or blowing, or how has it blown in the past? What trouble has come because of this storm?

Can you see God working to calm you or calm the storm, helping you to trust Him in it? How do you know that He is God and R.E.S.T. (*refuge, ever*-present *strength* in *trouble*) in that truth? How or where do you see His help?

READY TO R.E.S.T.?

READ AND REFLECT: What do the Scriptures and this Bible study say about storms of sickness? What do they say about Jesus, your refuge in this storm? What were your biggest takeaways?

EXAMINE QUESTIONS AND EXPLORE ANSWERS: For greater understanding and for application, seek answers in Scripture and meditate upon the personal questions.

SHARE: Tell about your takeaways and your storm, with a group or alone, as you write or pray about them.

TRUST your Refuge, the One who provides *relationship* and *remedy*.

STORMS OF SHAME

THE SAMARITAN WOMAN—
JOHN 4:3–30, 39–42

DAY 1: BUFFETED BY THE STORM

WHEN YOU CAN'T CATCH YOUR BREATH

Because I grew up in the Great Plains, I know wind—blow-you-over, knock-you-down, sometimes-straight-line wind. Combine the wind with heavy rain or snow, and you have yourself a whiteout or a blizzard. Now envision walking into it. You simply cannot catch your breath or move forward, because the weather pelts you and takes your breath away. It's accurate to say you're being buffeted by the storm.

What happens in life when you are buffeted by a storm of regrets, failures, or mistakes? They fly in your face until you can't catch your breath. Maybe you regularly pelt yourself with thoughts such as these: "The hurt I caused is unforgivable." "I'm not worthy of anyone's respect." "If they knew what I did, they would call me a hypocrite." "Who do I think I am to try? I'm a failure."

If even one of these statements caused you to wince, perhaps you have been buffeted by the storms of shame too.

There's more. Between my own admissions and those of others, I have a list of shame points blowing your way:

- I've carried shame for something done to me.

- I have hidden sins I don't want anyone to know about.

- I've been trapped in a bad habit that produced pain to myself and others.

- I'm embarrassed by secret thoughts I sometimes have.

- I've brought shame to my family because of my choices.

- I have made unscrupulous decisions and have brought shame upon myself.

- I made regrettable decisions, yesterday and twenty years ago.

Is a failure, a hidden sin, or a regret preventing you from catching your breath, from living life fully? Satan loves to have us dwell on every shortcoming and secret sin, such as that unethical task we undertook, that terrible thing we did to you-know-who, or that lie we told that wrecked a relationship. In my book *Stepping Out*, I wrote, "The enemy would have us constantly looking back over our shoulder, peering into the past, focusing on our former sins, failures, and regrets. He may even whisper such lies as 'You will never get over this. You will always struggle with that past sin holding you captive. Just give up. After all you have done, God could never forgive you, and neither could anyone else.' "[50]

In our weaker moments, we may feel that our regrettable decisions prohibit us from living or deserving a respectable life. This is when we are buffeted by storms of shame. They blow so hard that they threaten to take us out.

> **R&R:** What storms of shame have buffeted you? Tell them to the Lord as you take a look at the storm of a woman from the little village of Sychar in Samaria.

A WOMAN'S STORM OF SHAME—BASED ON JOHN 4:3–30, 39–42

The woman walked alone to the well, balancing a clay jar on her shoulder. She was going to draw water. The other women from her village would have long-since returned to their homes; they wouldn't venture back here until the cool of the evening. They scorned her, so she waited until the sun was high in the sky and the well was deserted to go for water. Shame beat down on her like the noonday sun as she recalled their pointing fingers and whispers, and considered the reason for their actions.

Yet this day was different. As she drew near the well, she noticed a stranger—not a Samaritan, but a Jewish man—sitting by Himself. (The robe of a rabbi was a giveaway.) While Jacob's well was a common stopping place for thirsty travelers going through Samaria, prejudice and distrust existed between Jews and Samaritans. Many Jews avoided the direct route through the land, so why had He come?

As the woman began to draw water from the well, the man spoke to her: "Give Me a drink" (John 4:7). She was stunned. What had just happened? A man—a rabbi, no less—dared to speak to a Samaritan woman. Didn't He know He was breaking the rules of culture, gender, and religion?

The woman said, "How is it that You, a Jew, ask for a drink from me, a woman of Samaria?" (verse 9). "Jesus answered her, 'If you knew the gift of God, and who it is that is saying to you, "Give Me a drink," you would have asked Him, and He would have given you living water' " (verse 10).

How could He offer water without so much as a cup to dip into the deep well? Where would this man get what He called "living water"? Her questions spilled before Him. Then He replied, "Everyone who drinks of this water will be thirsty again, but whoever drinks of the water that I will give him will never be thirsty again. The water that I will give him will become in him a spring of water welling up to eternal life" (verses 13–14).

Water that would forever quench thirst? No more lonely trips to the well, daily reminders of her shame and the scorn to which she was subjected? She blurted out, "Sir, give me this water, so that I will not be thirsty or have to come here to draw water" (verse 15).

"Go, call your husband, and come here," the man said (verse 16). Of course, He would assume she was married. How could He possibly know her sordid marital past? She stated a simple fact: "I have no husband" (verse 17). Would her shame be evident in her voice?

The man replied, "You are right in saying, 'I have no husband'; for you have had five husbands, and the one you now have is not your husband. What you have said is true" (verses 17–18). His answer was baffling. He had an inexplicable knowledge of her life. It was clear that He knew. But He didn't speak to her with condescension or condemnation. He seemed to be peering into her heart, as if He also knew her needs, perhaps better than she did.

She had been treated as a possession. She longed for love, was desperate to attract another man's attention when the last had left her. She was desperate for protection and provision too. She rationalized what she had done as a way to survive. And now this man looked at her in a whole new way, radically different than any man had before. Certainly, there were no innuendos. But there were no sneers either, and nothing to indicate judgment.

Clearly this was no ordinary man. He must be a prophet of God. "Sir, I perceive that You are a prophet" (verse 19). But wait. If He was a Jewish prophet, why would He have concern for a Samaritan woman?

Jesus' reply broke a barrier, revealing much about the Father, salvation, and true worship. The Samaritan woman had knowledge of her people's history; she knew that Jacob was her ancestor too. She also knew that a great prophet, the Messiah, had been promised. Could this be Him? "I know that Messiah is coming (He who is called Christ). When He comes, He will tell us all things," she said (verse 25).

"I who speak to you am He" (verse 26). He spoke just a few words, but they were earth-shattering, life-changing words. They must be true. This man knew her past. He spoke with certainty about the future. He said everything with an authority such as she had never heard before. He offered her living water, faith, and eternal life. These were gifts only the promised Messiah could give.

Her heart leapt! The man who stood before her was the promised One, the Messiah Himself! He had come to her, just as she was. He told her what she had done—and He extended forgiveness and offered salvation.

Still stunned, she saw more Jews approaching. They appeared to be with Him. Their surprised glances in her direction as they greeted Jesus revealed their thoughts. (Why would Jesus speak with a Samaritan woman?) Suddenly, she knew what she must do. She turned and ran toward the town, nearly bursting with newfound courage and an urgent need to speak of her life-giving discovery. In her haste, she left behind the jar she'd come to fill.

With joy and conviction, she shouted, "Come, see a man who told me all that I ever did. Can this be the Christ?" (verse 29). No longer buffeted by the storm of her shame, but filled instead with living water, she could not contain the Messiah's message. Through this divine encounter, Jesus quenched her thirst as only He could!

Would they believe the testimony of a woman such as her? Leaning in, not only did they listen but they also were eager to discover more about this man for themselves. When they found Jesus and had their own encounters with Him, they proclaimed, "We know that this is indeed the Savior of the world" (verse 42).

> **R&R:** Ponder the story of the Samaritan woman's storm as you read John 4:3–30, 39–42. Write what stood out to you. What was your first and immediate takeaway?

DISCUSSION QUESTION 1 "God is our refuge and strength, a very present help in trouble" (Psalm 46:1). In what ways did Jesus fulfill these words of the psalmist for this woman? How was He her refuge in her storm of shame?

Buffeted by her storm, the woman at the well sought only drinking water. She received, instead, the water of eternal life, *refreshment* provided freely to her by Jesus. She could be still and know that He is God, her Savior from sin and shame, her *rescuer*!

DISCUSSION QUESTION 2 "Be still, and know that I am God. I will be exalted among the nations, I will be exalted in the earth!" (Psalm 46:10). Picture this woman's life following her encounter with Christ. How do you think these words would have spoken to her? How was Jesus exalted in her life and through her?

Know that you are not beyond rescue from your storm either. He is with you. He is your strength. Be still and know that He is God, incomparably greater than your storm.

JOURNAL: What one takeaway today enables me to say, "I can be still because I know that He is God"?

DAY 2: HE KNOWS

IN THE HEAT OF THE DAY

As I write this, the sun beats down on me in my backyard, and I remind myself to hydrate. How quickly we become parched under the sun. Even a leisurely day under the hot summer rays wears me out. How about you? Try trekking many miles by foot in the heat of the day. The need for rest and refuel was real for Jesus and His disciples during a long journey from Judea to Galilee.

GEOGRAPHY AND BACKDROP

Jesus was likely alone as He sat down to rest, "wearied as He was from His journey" (John 4:6), while His disciples went further to buy food. Few others would have come to the well in the heat of the day, yet an unnamed woman appeared. This was no surprise to Jesus as He entered the stormy darkness of her world.

Samaria sat between Judea to the south and Galilee to the north. Many Jews who traveled from one to the other preferred to cross the Jordan river, covering Gentile ground, rather than travel the direct route and step foot on Samaritan soil, since the Israelites despised the Samaritans and considered them unclean.[51]

Jesus "had to pass through Samaria" (verse 4) only because God had a plan. Centuries earlier, a civil war had torn the kingdom of Israel in two. The Northern Kingdom repeatedly fell into idolatry, and God allowed the Assyrians to conquer it. They brought in foreigners and carried off those they captured, leaving the remaining Jews to intermarry with their new neighbors. The result was a mixed racial group named for the region in which they lived: Samaria.[52] Many Samaritans knew the laws and religion of their ancestors, but in the eyes of pure Jews, the Samaritans had lost their right to be called Jews. Both regions were now under Roman rule, so they were loosely connected again in an uneasy union. Jews considered Samaritans unclean, so the fear of contamination was another reason they commonly traveled the long way around. Additionally, passing through "could lead to a hostile encounter."[53] Moreover, it was culturally prohibitive for a Jewish rabbi to speak publicly with a woman at all.

DISCUSSION QUESTION 1 Based on what you just read, how would you expect to be treated by a Jewish rabbi if you were a Samaritan woman? List the reasons a Jew might avoid going through Samaria altogether.

DISCUSSION QUESTION 2 Jesus ignored the hostility between Jews and Samaritans and the condescending attitude toward women. Can you pinpoint what Jesus was willing to do that would defile Him, according to Mosaic Law?[54]

"IF YOU KNEW THE GIFT OF GOD" (JOHN 4:10)

The woman at the well needed to know the who and what of this "living water" that is "the gift of God": Jesus, and eternal life in Him for all who believe. The Greek word for "gift" (*dorea*) "emphasizes God's grace through Christ."[55] To drink of the living water is to believe in Him for salvation and eternal life. Jesus knew the worst of her: the long list of broken marriages, the series of bad choices, the sexual immorality. And still He chose her; He led her to living water. He invited her to receive His grace, which fully covered her shame and her deeds, her past and her pain.

DISCUSSION QUESTION 3 Define *gift* in a broad sense. Now place the Greek definition of *dorea* beside it. What is so significant about Jesus' choice of words here regarding God's offer?

At first, it seems that Jesus changed the subject as soon as the woman asked for the water He offered. Moreover, why would Jesus ask her to call her husband if He already knew her past and current situations? With empathy and compassion, He was drawing into the light what she had held in darkness. He was bringing into the open what she would have kept in secret. By exposing the truth and His knowledge of it, He enabled her to see her sin and come to repentance so healing could begin.

DISCUSSION QUESTION 4 Jesus exposed the truth. What made His revelation of her life radically different? If those who knew her had exposed her that day, how would their treatment have been different? Note the progression that began by enabling her to see her sin. What followed? What happened to her shame? How does that apply to Jesus' work in your life too?

THE ANTIDOTE TO SHAME

Look back at the list of shame statements in yesterday's reading. Then consider the shame of the Samaritan woman's situation. Do you see a common denominator? On some level, they all contain judgment, silence, or secrecy. According to Brené Brown, author, speaker, and research professor at the University of Houston, shame needs these three things to thrive. During an acclaimed TED Talk, Brown said, "Shame is an epidemic in our culture, and to get out from underneath it, to find our way back to each other, we have to understand how it affects us. . . . We have to understand and know empathy, because empathy is the antidote to shame."[56]

DISCUSSION QUESTION 5 Based on what we know, how had shame affected the woman in Samaria? How does shame affect you? Why might empathy or compassion be considered an antidote to shame?

My friend Stacey, a director of Christian education, ministers to youth, families, and young adults. She wonders, with a heart of compassion:

> How many believers are living in isolation, and also without deep spiritual community? We all want to be known, but we don't know how to be in authentic Christian community with each other. We have issues with being vulnerable because there is a pressure to look perfect. Fear of judgment keeps us from being vulnerable. "Can you love me for who I am really am? Can you love my yuck?" We should be asking each other real questions, like, "What's your faith story?" "How is God messing with your heart?" Let's create a safe place of empathy. Let's ask the questions. Let's get the conversations going.[57]

R&R: Have you felt the pressure to be perfect? Are there people with whom you can be vulnerable and authentic? What kinds of real questions do you ask one another to get the conversations going?

With God's help, we can let down our protective walls of isolation, behind which we harbor secrets or sit in silent judgment and shame. With the walls down, we can be vulnerable and real with one another and with the Lord. We can learn compassion and empathy for ourselves and for others as we connect on a deeper, authentic level. Jesus' knowledge, care, and compassion for the woman at the well—unique, personal, and empathetic—opened the door to trust, faith, and a saving relationship.

DISCUSSION QUESTION 6 There is nothing your Savior does not know about you. Read Psalm 94:11; Psalm 139:1–4; Acts 1:24; Luke 12:6–7, 29–31 for comforting reminders. What examples are given? How does knowing this comfort you? How do these verses help you to be vulnerable and honest with Him? How do they increase your thirst for a closer walk with Him?

JOURNAL: What one takeaway today enables me to say, "I can be still because I know that He is God"?

DAY 3: WHY HE CAME AND WHAT HE SEEKS

MORE TO THE STORY?

I was quick to judge another mother when I overheard some harsh words she had for her kids. "Shame on you for speaking to them that way," I thought, as I silently pronounced a sentence upon her: she must be a bad mom. I was chagrined to learn later that this was uncharacteristic for her and that she had later apologized to her children, allowing God to use the situation and her confession to provide a teachable moment for the entire family.

How often do we judge someone at first glance, when there is always more to the story? Even when we think we have all the facts, our view is still limited and may be biased. "I'm a good judge of character," we might say. But wait; back up. That statement implies that we have judged someone. It's true that we are known by our fruit (Luke 6:44) and that outward actions may reflect the character within, but we are called to let God alone be the judge of another person. When we're quick to condemn, we are failing to see the person we are condemning with eyes of compassion. Can we simply see her as another flawed human being, such as ourselves, also in need of a Savior? Do we remember she is also covered in God's grace? As we discussed in yesterday's study, compassion can go a long way toward removing shame and may even help create change.

Had the Samaritan woman made one unscrupulous decision after another? The simple facts point to that, but there may have been more to her story. It was not uncommon for a woman to become widowed and then remarry. Five times, however, was unlikely. Divorce was almost never initiated by a woman, but Mosaic Law allowed a man to divorce his wife in a variety of situations (see Deuteronomy 24:1). It is also possible that she was abandoned by one or more husbands.

Her circumstances beg the question: was she terribly mistreated or of moral question? It's possible that both were backdrops to her current living situation. "We don't know why she had so many husbands, but we can be sure she had suffered as a result. . . . Jesus did not dwell on her sin (or ignore it)."[58] Jesus didn't ask her to explain her past or discuss reasons for the roads she had taken. He didn't ask her to explain her current living situation. Nor did He reason with her that she may have been seeking escape, providing an excuse for the life she lived.

> **R&R:** Maybe you have heard the story of Jesus and the Samaritan woman several times. Have you ever wondered if there may have been more to her story? Do suppositions diminish or worsen her storm in any way?

DISCUSSION QUESTION 1 Jesus did not dwell on the woman's sin, nor did He ignore it. He knew everything about her, and He knew her heart. He didn't ask for explanation or look for an excuse from her. What He did do was approach her with forgiveness and grace. What can we learn from His approach?

We may blame our circumstances on others or justify our actions that led to shame. But blame-shifting or excusing our actions doesn't lead us down the road of repentance. Our Savior leads us down this healing path, surrounded by His grace.

DISCUSSION QUESTION 2 Why do you think Jesus chose to come to the Samaritan woman? What did He know about her? What did He want her to know about Him amid her storm? How did He show that He cared about both her daily life and her spiritual life?

The Samaritan woman found her refuge in Jesus' *rescue*! He redeemed her from the storm of shame, and He provided her with eternal *refreshment* in His living water.

DISCUSSION QUESTION 3 Why has Jesus chosen to come to you? What does He know about you? What does He want you to know about Him amid your storms of shame? How has He shown that He cares about both your daily life and your spiritual life?

Shame can cause us to retreat and avoid others. It can also cause us to ignore God and His Word, certain that He will only condemn us. We know all too well our secrets and regrettable decisions. Satan would have us believe we are beyond hope, beyond forgiveness. When I wrote *Stepping Out* several years ago, I pondered my own past, especially the places where I had been shamed by someone else or had slapped that label upon myself. As God healed me, I was able to respond with these words: "My former failures do not dictate who I am today. The sins of my past [fully forgiven!] do not . . . *de*fine me, but God can use those rough spots to *re*fine me as He shapes me continually into His Son's image."[59] These words ring true today too. I am a forgiven child of God, and so are you. There is always more to our story, as God continues His refining work in us.

R&R: Have you ever allowed your feelings of shame to send you into retreat mode? Have you ever been led to believe that certain decisions define you? Reminded of your true identity in Christ, how can you see His refining work in you?

We find refuge in His *rescue*! He redeemed us from the storm of shame. He provides *refreshment* in His living water, today and eternally.

TRUE WORSHIP

"You worship what you do not know; we worship what we know, for salvation is from the Jews" (John 4:22). "The Samaritan Bible contained only the [Books of Moses]. [Samaritans] worshiped the true God, but their failure to accept much of his revelation meant that they knew little of Him."[60]

"But the hour is coming, and is now here, when the true worshipers will worship the Father in spirit and truth, for the Father is seeking such people to worship Him. God is spirit, and those who worship Him must worship in spirit and truth" (verses 23–24). Jesus didn't debate the place of worship, because His salvation work was changing everything! "The hour was simultaneously coming and present, since Christ was in the midst of accomplishing everything the Father had sent Him to do."[61] What would matter was faith in God. Beyond all cultural boundaries and roadblocks stood the one true God, calling this woman to faith. She received a new understanding of Him: He was her Lord too!

DISCUSSION QUESTION 4 God seeks you and me, as He did this woman, that we may be true worshipers. According to verses 23–24, what kind of worship and worshiper is God seeking?

We worship in faith, by the Holy Spirit's power, and in truth centered on the Word made flesh: Jesus Christ, "the way, and the truth, and the life" (John 14:6). Over and over in the Gospel of John, truth is associated with Christ Himself. "When the truth of Jesus Christ reaches our souls and God's Spirit touches ours so that we believe, true worship begins. We don't merely go through the motions of worship. Our whole being is involved."[62] True worship is also anchored in God's Word of truth; Scripture is proclaimed. In worship, we praise God: Father, Son, and Holy Spirit. We confess our sin, repent of it, and receive absolution. We rejoice in God's grace and believe in Jesus' sacrifice for the forgiveness of sins and eternal life.

JOURNAL: What one takeaway today enables me to say, "I can be still because I know that He is God"?

DAY 4: RESCUED FROM SHAME

SEARCH AND RESCUE

When we receive news that a search-and-rescue team has been organized, we know someone is in trouble and in need of prayer. Maybe a boat has been capsized in stormy waves or a plane has gone down in a thunderstorm. Emergency crews are deployed, and a search for survivors begins. The goal is simple: to rescue every survivor and bring him or her to safety.

As we continue to study the story of the Samaritan woman, we find that a successful search-and-rescue attempt was taking place. Here the woman was the one who was searching. Jesus was the one who rescued her.

COME, SEE!

The Samaritan woman arrived at the well in search of water and anonymity, but she walked away (or rather, ran) with something she had unknowingly searched for her entire life: living water. Rescued and released, she was so excited that she left her water jar at the well and headed straight for town with the news.

> **R&R:** What is significant about the mention of the water jar the woman left behind? When have you gone in search of one thing, only to find another, and then realized that what you found was better than you hoped for? Share.

The rescued woman ran from her encounter with the Lord as an evangelist to the same people who had shamed and shunned her. Nearly as amazing as her testimony was the townspeople's response to it. We might think they wouldn't listen to the ill-reputed woman, but she spoke so boldly of the long-awaited Messiah that they had to "come, see" for themselves (John 4:29)!

The first words of the woman's report were not, "I have received living water." She spoke, instead, of Jesus' knowledge of her life: He "told me all that I ever did" (verse 29). Then she invited them to come and see Him for themselves. Have we considered that the best way to approach someone with the Good News of Christ is simply to tell our story? Do we share our personal Good News? "He knows my sins and my shame. He met me right where I was and rescued me! He gave me forgiveness and eternal life! Who is He? The Christ! You have to come and see—meet Him for yourselves!" When she said, "Can this be the Christ?" (verse 29), it was not so much a question as it was a testimony of hope and joy.

> **R&R:** Tell your story. Go ahead. Prepare to tell the Good News, as shared through your faith story. Others will want to come and see!

Because of the woman's testimony, many people met Jesus that day. Through one forgiven woman, the Lord brought many to receive His free gift of faith. Although we don't know what became of her, we trust that her life was never the same. Gone was the shame of the past that once held her captive. Forgiven and free, she received the life-giving refreshment that comes only through Christ. Jesus "makes her a believer and a witness, and she enjoys a witness's reward; her fellow townsmen come to Jesus, prevail on Him to stay with them, and find in Him the Savior who . . . excludes no one from salvation, the *Savior of the world.*"[63]

SHAME ON YOU

Maybe something has happened to make you think you're unworthy. The Jews thought the Samaritans were unworthy. The people of Sychar thought this woman unworthy. But Jesus dispelled both thoughts. He came to save all people, and these Samaritans, adversaries of the Jews, were some of the first people to believe that.

DISCUSSION QUESTION 1 Have you fallen prey to believing that you shouldn't have enjoyed something good that came your way? Did you think you didn't deserve it because of this or that reason?

A FAILED ATTEMPT

Happy to have a plan for self-discipline, my friend Carol began a Lenten forty-day fast from social media. How did it go? Not so well. Carol was embarrassed to report that only a week into the fast, she had already weakened. Carol admitted:

> I faltered . . . when I posted about my son and a school event. That then turned into a "quick" look through my feed, which led to a longer look and several more posts. Until eventually, I was swept up into the current events and wanting to stay connected with what was going on and how everyone was doing [during the 2020 COVID crisis].

My feelings of hope and my anticipated "success" in completing my Lenten discipline turned into feelings of defeat and anxiousness. I felt I had failed. And as I struggled to reconcile this perceived failure over the following few weeks, Christ reminded me that the completion of the discipline itself was not the point. The point was the One I met when I stumbled and fell. The One I turned to with my regret and frustration. ["The steps of a man are established by the LORD, when he delights in His way; though he fall, he shall not be cast headlong, for the LORD upholds his hand" (Psalm 37:23–24).] It wasn't about what I accomplished but about Christ working within me to remind me of my great need for Him. And that is not just a 40-day journey but an everyday, life-long practice. . . . [I can] stand firm in His goodness and strength, knowing that [my] worth is in Him.[64]

DISCUSSION QUESTION 2 We may feel embarrassment, regret, and shame when we fall short. How comforting to know that when our steps are established by the Lord, we will not be "cast headlong" when we fall (Psalm 37:24). Why not, according to Psalm 37:24? In His grace, God might have a different purpose for the plan we meant to undertake. Using Carol's story as an example, when have you experienced something similar? How did you see Him working in you?

Don't confuse shame with guilt. Guilt says, "You messed up," but shame says, "You're a mess-up." Guilt says, "You made a mistake," but shame says, "You're a mistake." Guilt says, "You failed that attempt," but shame says, "You're a failure." Pastor Michael Newman put it this way:

> Guilt says you did something wrong, but shame declares that you are undeserving of being loved and unworthy of being blessed. Shame wants you to believe that nothing good or fulfilling or joyful or right should be in your life. Why? Because, shame alleges, you're not good enough for that.[65]

In your shame, maybe you're convinced that something you've done, said, or thought is beyond the bounds of forgiveness, both from others and from God.

SHAME OFF YOU!

Jesus comes to you when you are swept up in a storm of shame that you think there's no getting out of it. He pursues you and sweeps you up in a completely different way, replacing shame with His grace. He chooses you and calls you His own; He embraces you in His love, no matter your track record. Relief comes as you recognize the difference between guilt and shame. With honesty and vulnerability, admit and confess your sins to the Lord. Jesus says, "Shame *off* you!" He rescues you from the storm and restores you to a right relationship with God. He removes the shame, and He sends you out to serve, refreshed with His living water and ready to shout what He has done for you!

> **R&R:** Practice and personalize your understanding of the difference between guilt and shame. Remember the difference: guilt condemns your sin, now forgiven in Christ. Shame continues to condemn you.

Know that you cannot be held hostage by shame, because you are forgiven in Christ. He comes to you, offering His gift of grace. He gives you the same unmerited, undeserved favor He offered to the Samaritan woman at the well. God is bigger than your biggest storms!

DISCUSSION QUESTION 3 Maybe the aftermath of a storm has left you stuck in the mud. Trust in the One who lifts you from it. Where does He set you instead (see Psalm 40:2)? Where is this rock? Read 1 Corinthians 10:4; Ephesians 2:20.

> **R&R:** How might the Lord use your story of rescue from past shame to help you minister to someone today? How can you remind that person that Jesus says, "Shame off you?" How is your capacity for empathy impacted by your own story?

JOURNAL: What one takeaway today enables me to say, "I can be still because I know that He is God"?

DAY 5: REFRESHED!

LIVING WATER

Hydration is paramount to the body's survival. How long can we live without food or water? We last a little longer without food: generally speaking, about three weeks. But without water, we would only last about three to four days.[66]

DISCUSSION QUESTION 1 How necessary is water? What about living water? What does the psalmist say about thirst in Psalm 42:1–2? What do we read about living water in Jeremiah 2:13?

> There is a river whose streams make glad the city of God, the holy habitation of the Most High. (Psalm 46:4)

Springs of life-giving water flow from Jesus,[67] the "river whose streams make glad the city of God." At the heart of the city of God is her living water, Christ Jesus. His life-giving refreshment makes His people glad! The city of God, where the Most High dwells in His holy habitation, is now within His people, the new Jerusalem, all believers in Christ.[68] We can be still and know that He is God; He is in our midst and is filling us with life-giving living water.

DISCUSSION QUESTION 2 The living water Jesus offered to the woman at the well was the metaphoric picture of the gift He provides to all who believe: eternal life. Just a few chapters later, in John 7:37–39, we see Jesus expound further. Read this passage and note where the rivers of living water flow. Specifically, what is the living water Jesus refers to here? How do people receive it, so that it may flow from them?

SHAME, IN LIGHT OF LIVING WATER

In our shame, we are dry, parched, and weary, longing for something that will satisfy our thirst. This thirst won't be quenched any other way than by Christ. He comes to us, knowing just where we'll be and where we've been. He sees our parched lips, reveals our real thirst, and knows our weary soul's needs. He alone can remove our shame, satisfy our thirst, and save our sin-parched soul.

DISCUSSION QUESTION 3 What does God do for us, according to Psalm 31:1–2? "Let me never be put to shame; in Your righteousness deliver me! Incline Your ear to me; rescue me speedily! Be a rock of refuge for me, a strong fortress to save me!" Read it again, this time circling the words you have seen repeatedly in this session.

DISCUSSION QUESTION 4 You have been given new life in Christ! The old has gone; the new has come. Read Ephesians 4:20–32 and contrast the old with the new, created through God's work in you. Share several contrasting pairs of the old and the new. Which pair stands out to you?

> **R&R:** By God's grace, you are a new person. Because of this, do you hide pieces of your past that you're not so proud of? What would it take to be willing to share openly your story of Christ's work in you so others can see and benefit from it?

I have a friend who courageously shares her storm of shame. As you read her story below, you can't miss her authenticity and vulnerability, evidence of Christ's work in her. Strong in faith, refreshed by His living water, and overflowing with compassion and grace, she trusts that others will benefit from her story too.

HIS GRACE IS ENOUGH

Shame. It can take so much joy away from you. It leaves you with feelings of guilt and regret. When I was a junior in high school, I was dating someone who wasn't a Christian. At the time, I thought I was doing the right thing by trying to show him Jesus. But actually, it was hurting my relationship with God more than I knew. I eventually realized that we were unequally yoked and the relationship was bad for me, but I was so in "love" with him that I couldn't bring myself to leave the relationship. The devil takes advantage of people when they are most distant from God. I let my guard down and fell into temptation. Even though I wasn't having sex, I was still committing sexual sin, and it became a habit. I started to believe that it wasn't that bad, although I still felt shame about it. My boyfriend said that every other high school couple was doing it, so what could be wrong? I ended up having sex with him once.

Someone in my church told me to have a talk with him about how I felt, and if it didn't go well, I should break up with him. I knew this person was right, but I took the easy way out and continued to date him for eight more months. I still had hope that he might change. After this relationship ended, I realized how much it tore me away from God. I was lost and insecure without my boyfriend because I had put a great portion of my identity in him, instead of Christ.

I felt tremendous guilt and shame for years about it. I knew that my boyfriend meant no harm, so I often put all the blame on myself. I knew it was sin, but to him it was not. I didn't tell anyone about it until a year after it happened because it was not something I was proud of. I asked God for forgiveness, and I know that He forgave me, but sometimes I felt like my apology wasn't enough. I still felt dirty for what I did.

My next boyfriend was a Christian. I had learned from my mistake—one that I did not want to repeat, and it was not a mistake he wanted to make either. He encouraged me to strengthen my relationship with Christ. Even though I am no longer with this boyfriend, I know very well now that God is always with me. It is often very hard to be still and know that God has a plan. I know that I will have to be honest, take responsibility for my actions, and tell my future husband that I messed up, and if he is the right person for me, he will understand and forgive me too.

I have often wondered why God allowed me to fall into that temptation, but it has made me a stronger person. I know that I am pure, washed by Jesus' precious blood. I am forever grateful for God's unconditional love and grace. There is no sin so big that His grace cannot cover it, even though it may not always feel like it. There is no sin that wasn't paid for on His cross. His grace makes no sense, but that is what's so beautiful about it. What I hope people can learn from my story is that His grace is enough. We were not made to carry our burdens alone. We can always go to God with our struggles and weaknesses, our shame and regrets. He is for us, not against us. . . . And there is always forgiveness.[69]

My friend sought and received forgiveness, but initially she felt as if her apology wasn't enough. God continued to work in her, and through healthy relationships, vulnerable conversations, and growth in her faith, she is now stronger and more certain of God's forgiveness at Christ's cross. She is sure of His work through her to help others and of the message of His grace that she shares.

R&R: Recall a time when you let your guard down and fell into temptation. Maybe you thought the action wouldn't be all that bad. Maybe you placed a portion of your identity in something connected to the sin that brought you shame. Let my friend's message speak to your heart: His grace is enough. You do not carry your burden alone. Go to God. Be vulnerable with others. Rest in His forgiveness for you.

R&R: "God is our refuge and strength, a very present help in trouble" (Psalm 46:1). In light of all you've learned in this week's session, in what ways does Jesus fulfill these words of the psalmist for you? What does your Refuge's gift of *rescue* mean to you? What about the *refreshment* you receive from His living water, daily and eternally?

JOURNAL: What one takeaway today enables me to say, "I can be still because I know that He is God"?

VIEWER GUIDE

SESSION 4: STORMS OF SHAME

Turn to John 4:3–30, 39–42.

Jesus led the woman of Samaria to recognize Him:

• He was more than merely a tired, thirsty Jewish rabbi who _____ to ask a Samaritan woman for a drink.

• He was more than a mysterious stranger who _____ her sin and shame.

• He was more than someone who had a _____ to give.

• He was even more than a prophet who revealed a new and true _____ that would be for all people, by the gift of the Spirit.

• Jesus led her to a dawning recognition of Him as the _____, the Messiah, the promised _____ of the world.

Buffeted by her storm, the woman at the well sought drinking water and received, instead, the water of eternal life, _____ provided freely to her by Jesus. She could be still and know that He is God, her Savior from sin and shame, her _____.

Jesus does for you and me what He did for the woman of Samaria:

• He _____ to come to us in the midst of our shame.

• He is certainly no stranger, and He _____ our sin and shame.

• He has the greatest gift to give: eternally _____ living water.

• He leads us in true _____, in faith by the Holy Spirit.

• He enables us to recognize, receive, and believe in Him as _____, our _____!

DISCUSS

> God is our refuge and strength, a very present help in trouble. Therefore we will not fear though the earth gives way, though the mountains be moved into the heart of the sea, though its waters roar and foam, though the mountains tremble at its swelling. . . . "Be still, and know that I am God." (Psalm 46:1–3, 10)

As you consider your storms of shame, what do your roaring waters and trembling mountains look like? How is your storm brewing or blowing in a specific situation? What trouble has come because of this storm?

Can you see God working to calm you or calm the storm, helping you to trust Him in it? How do you know that He is God and R.E.S.T. (*refuge*, *ever*-present *strength* in *trouble*) in that truth? How or where do you see His help?

READY TO R.E.S.T.?

READ AND REFLECT: What do the Scriptures and this Bible study say about storms of shame? What do they say about Jesus, your refuge in this storm? What were your biggest takeaways?

EXAMINE QUESTIONS AND EXPLORE ANSWERS: For greater understanding and for application, seek answers in Scripture and meditate upon the personal questions.

SHARE: Tell about your takeaways and your storm, with a group or alone, as you write or pray about them.

TRUST your Refuge, the One who provides *rescue* and *refreshment*.

STORMS OF SCURRY

MARTHA OF BETHANY—LUKE 10:38–42

DAY 1: WHEN ACTION BECOMES DISTRACTION

MAY I SERVE YOU?

My friend Elizabeth has an incredible gift of hospitality. When she opens her home to serve, her guests are in for a treat, and not just the delectable kind. Elizabeth loves to cook, and she finds great pleasure in feeding all who enter her home. She has an eye for detail and a flair that enables her to take an average meal and give it amazing appeal. But more than that, Elizabeth makes her guests feel that her home is their home while they are under her roof. She shares her love for the Lord through this special act of service. Elizabeth also knows that the service itself can become a distraction. Since she relates with Martha, I've invited her to share a few insights. You will find them woven into the next two days' studies.

Serving others is a good thing. In fact, serving is a portion of our purpose. It's the action connected to the love we receive from God and then get to hand out in His name. Just turn to Ephesians 2 and you'll read a great reminder of God's call for our action. Ephesians 2:8 tells us we are saved from our sins solely by God's grace, through His gift of faith in Christ. What flows from this grace? The actions—the good works—for which He created us. "For we are His workmanship, created in Christ Jesus for good works, which God prepared beforehand, that we should walk in them" (Ephesians 2:10). But sometimes, actions become distractions.

> **R&R:** Our service is a good thing, but when might our actions become distractions? How may serving become bothersome? When could a flurry of service become a storm of scurry?

MARTHA'S STORM OF SCURRY—BASED ON LUKE 10:38–42

She could hardly contain herself. The Lord said yes to her invitation. He and His disciples were coming to her home to receive a meal at her table. How could she possibly honor Him adequately? Martha gave great thought to the preparations she would make for hosting Jesus in the home she shared with her sister, Mary, and her brother, Lazarus, in the town of Bethany.

As soon as she and her siblings welcomed their special guests, Martha scurried back to the hearth to complete the meal. There was so much to do, and she wanted it to be perfect. After all, Jesus wasn't just any guest. This traveling preacher and family friend was the talk of the region, performing miracles, teaching with authority, healing, and casting out demons! His messages were amazing—unlike anything they had heard. When He spoke about the kingdom of God, He gave hope and promised peace. Moreover, He had sought out her humble family, time and again; He called them friends! He and His band of followers relaxed noticeably from the rigors of ministry travels when they took off their sandals, washed their feet, and reclined in the comfort of her home. This day, not unlike others, they were bound to be hungry, so she hastened to finish the special meal.

The preparations were almost complete, and she needed more hands; it was a good thing Mary was there to help. But wait; where had Mary gone? Poking her head around the corner, Martha could hardly believe the scene before her. There sat Mary at Jesus' feet as He taught His disciples. With every passing moment, Martha's agitation grew. What did Mary think she was doing, joining the men's conversation? A woman's proper place was near the hearth, preparing and serving a meal. Martha was humiliated by her sister's inappropriate behavior, frustrated by her lack of help, and hurt that the Lord didn't appear to care; she was left alone to slave over the hearth and serve them all. Martha's anxiety escalated until she couldn't contain herself any longer. "Lord, do You not care that my sister has left me to serve alone? Tell her then to help me" (Luke 10:40).

Even as she blurted the words, Martha's frown was met by the Lord's loving gaze. Rich with compassion, Jesus' words of reply were not what she expected: "Martha, Martha, you are anxious and troubled about many things, but one thing is necessary. Mary has chosen the good portion, which will not be taken away from her" (verses 41–42).

"Martha, Martha." She had known from childhood that when her loved ones sought to convey their affection or sympathy, they would speak the name twice, endearingly.

She knew at once that He did care, so much more than she had realized during her short-sighted outburst. Jesus valued her service, to be sure. He knew her heart; He spoke straight into her hurt and frustration. He knew that she was, indeed, anxious and troubled about many things. In her overeager desire to serve, to manage her home, she'd tried to manage Mary and even Jesus. In response, He gently invited her to a place of peace that would begin at His feet.

> R&R: Pause to ponder the story of Martha's storm, also reading Luke 10:38–42. Then write what stood out to you. What was your first and immediate takeaway?

DISCUSSION QUESTION 1 "God is our refuge and strength, a very present help in trouble" (Psalm 46:1). In what ways did Jesus fulfill these words of the psalmist for Martha? How was He her refuge in her storm of scurry?

In a storm of activity, Martha asked for assistance but received, instead, the opportunity to *rest*, to find respite in Him, along with gentle *redirection* to sit first at His feet.

DISCUSSION QUESTION 2 "Be still, and know that I am God. I will be exalted among the nations, I will be exalted in the earth!" (Psalm 46:10). Picture Martha's life following her encounter with Christ. How do you think these words would have spoken to her? How was Jesus exalted in her life and through her?

Jesus is with you. He is your Refuge and your Strength. Be still, and know that He is God, incomparably greater than your storm of scurry.

JOURNAL: What one takeaway today enables me to say, "I can be still because I know that He is God"?

DAY 2: EXPECT SOME REST

SERVICE WITH A SMILE

I can only imagine having the Lord Himself in my home for dinner. To be sure, I invite Him to be my guest, praying over every meal as I begin, mindful of His presence and thankful for His provision. But I marvel at the thought of serving Him a meal from my humble kitchen. I would want it to be the best.

Hospitality is a God-given directive. When Martha received Jesus and His disciples as her guests, she extended warm hospitality to them. She may have been preparing a meal for dozens of people that day.[70] Jesus speaks frequently about the importance of serving. His greatest purpose, that of coming to us to save us, was the ultimate form of service. He reminds His disciples, "The Son of Man came not to be served but to serve, and to give His life as a ransom for many" (Matthew 20:28). He also calls us to imitate Him in our service to others (John 13:15).

DISCUSSION QUESTION 1 Collectively, what do the following verses say about hospitality and serving? Read Galatians 5:13; 1 Peter 4:9–11; Colossians 3:23–24. What do you learn about serving from these texts?

Consider the reality of Martha's situation: the meal was not going to serve itself; someone needed to prepare and serve it. We know that our sympathetic Savior fully appreciated Martha's service. He and His followers relied on the provision and generosity of those among whom He ministered.[71]

Let me say this another way: Jesus was not criticizing Martha for her service. He did not scold or embarrass her either. In fact, He didn't address the service itself, but how she felt. Jesus knew Martha's mind and heart, her attitude behind her service, and that she was comparing her service to Mary's. Jesus did not dismiss her concern. In fact, He revealed His concern for her when He defined her feelings with His choice of words: anxious and troubled.

> **R&R:** When you're struggling with your feelings, how does it feel to have someone compassionately name them, making it clear she or he seeks to understand? Jesus, alone, can fully do this.

The Greek word *merimnao*, meaning "anxious" or "worried,"[72] is the same word Jesus used when He comforted His disciples, telling them not to worry about food, clothing, provision, or life, for the Father knew their needs (Luke 12:22–31). Anxiety can be a stumbling block to serving.

"Troubled" or "bothered" (from the Greek word *thorubeo*) refers to emotions spun out of control or to an uproar, such as that of an angry crowd.[73] Martha had worked herself into an upset frenzy.

"Distracted" (from the Greek word *perispao*) means "to drag all around."[74] Yes, "Martha was distracted with much serving" (verse 40). In her over-occupation with her service, she was dragging it around, crowding out that which truly fills. Meanwhile, Mary sat at the Lord's feet.

> **R&R:** *Anxious. Troubled. Distracted.* Take another look at the meaning of each word. To which can you relate most closely? Explain.

Martha knew Jesus well enough that she was confident she could approach Him with her concerns. We can commend her for trusting her concerns to her Lord, her friend. We know that this family had become close friends of Jesus. In John 11:5, we read, "Now Jesus loved Martha and her sister and Lazarus." This may not have been the first time He and others had reclined in her home, and we know it wouldn't be the last (see John 12). In *The Heart of Jesus,* author Marlys Taege Moberg wrote, "Jesus' response to Martha was caring, but firm. It reoriented Martha's priorities and reaffirmed Mary's—and it taught us something about our Savior's main concerns."[75]

> **R&R:** Do you need a nudge to know that you can confidently take your concerns to the Lord? Here is your nudge! What if your concern contains agitation, anger, or anxiety?

He knows your heart already. He sees you in your self-inflicted storm. He wants you to come to Him, to confess your concerns, your agitations, or your distractions, so that you may seek His help. "Cast your burden on the LORD, and He will sustain you" (Psalm 55:22). He desires to give you His direction (or redirection) in His Word, by His grace, and through His Spirit within you.

GREAT EXPECTATIONS

Elizabeth shared:

> Martha gets a lot of flak for her busyness. I very much relate to Martha and have to hold myself back from doing "one more thing" to make the experience "perfect" (I'm the only one who notices, anyway!). Jesus said, "[You are anxious and troubled about many things]" (verse 41). Details are often what drive us into a flurry of activity or distract us from the very thing we need to focus on: being there for our guests. That's what hospitality is—living a life of welcome for those around us. If our work leads to so many details that we have nothing left for the people, it's not worth it.
>
> I have struggled with the story of Mary and Martha over the years, because I usually hear, "Martha is wrong and Mary is right," which is basically true. But what if you have a Martha heart and you love the details, preparations, and service? That's not a problem. But it becomes a problem when the details overwhelm you, upset you, and take your attention off the greater purpose. When guests arrive and all you can think about is when will they leave (so you can rest), you know the details and the distractions have gotten the best of you.[76]

Like Martha, we have servant hearts. We are privileged to serve others in our homes and elsewhere. We can relate with Martha in her scurry, can't we? We want only the best for our guests. And like Martha, we become "distracted with much serving" (verse 40). We carry so much responsibility, and we have such great expectations. Stressed by the flurry of preparations on our path and caught in a storm of self-pity, we may find ourselves complaining like Martha: "Lord, don't You care that I have a commitment every night this week? Why isn't my husband helping me? Make others take notice and pick up the slack!"

As if life isn't already complicated enough, we make it even more complex by our choices. Have you ever felt overwhelmed by your daily routine? What do you expect from yourself on a given day? What do you expect from others? Are you seizing the day in such a way that you have a stranglehold on it in your attempt to control all the details, your actions, and the actions of others?

DISCUSSION QUESTION 2 What were Martha's expectations of herself after her guests arrived? What did she expect of Mary, and of Jesus? When you are "distracted with much serving," what expectations do you have of yourself? What do you expect of others?

Martha became hurried, harried, angry, frustrated, and distracted. Her resultant reactions were causally related to the choices she had made. Likewise, our reactions reflect our choices.

> **R&R:** It's wise to reevaluate and assess your commitments regularly. Where do you spend your time? What do you spend it doing? How many details are you juggling? After assessing, give yourself permission to rest.

Jesus invites us to make time for rest at His feet today. Just as He said to His disciples, He says to you and me, "Come away by yourselves to a desolate place and rest a while" (Mark 6:31). In your Savior's care, you can expect some rest.

JOURNAL: What one takeaway today enables me to say, "I can be still because I know that He is God"?

DAY 3: OF GREATEST IMPORTANCE

CALLED BY NAME

Like most wedding days, mine was filled with a flurry of activity: final details, decorations, and preparations. Since I was the bride *and* wedding planner, I thought I had to manage every last detail. Yes, I had created my own private storm of scurry. I was anything but still.

My beloved and I had chosen not to see each other until the ceremony, so our attendants kept us from an accidental encounter amid all the coming and going. Then it happened. In one unforgettable moment, my storm stopped. Though he couldn't see me, Cory called from behind closed doors, "Hi, Deb!" Suddenly, nothing else mattered. I was about to marry the man who called my name and calmed my storm with two words.

MARTHA, MARTHA

In Martha's flurry of activity, details, and preparations, she was anything but still. Jesus called to her in her private storm of scurry, and in one unforgettable moment, her storm stopped. Jesus called her by name and reminded her that one thing tops all others for time and priority. "Martha, Martha, you are anxious and troubled about many things, but one thing is necessary" (verses 41–42). It's significant that Jesus' repetition of her name implied pity, familiarity, and affection,[77] calming her storm as He did.

DISCUSSION QUESTION 1 When you are rattled, stop to imagine Jesus' tender words of redirection to you, beginning as He repeats your name. Write it here, two times: "_____, _____, you are anxious and troubled about many things, but only one thing is necessary. Sit at My feet. Be still, and know that I am God."

Take a look at Luke 13:34 and Luke 22:31, in which Jesus repeats a name out of pity or tender affection. What is the context? Is there a related storm involved?

DISCUSSION QUESTION 2 What is the one thing necessary? Jesus, the living Word! We receive His very words for faith, knowledge, and insight when we sit at His feet. We grow as we learn, understand, and receive His wisdom. What do these verses say about God's Word and our growth?

Philippians 2:16

Colossians 3:16

2 Peter 3:18

Our Savior comes to us in these storms of our own making, in the whirlwind of activity that can easily keep us from putting first things first. "Service that bypasses the Word is one that will never have lasting character. . . . Hearing God's Word must be our first priority."[78] We can approach Him with great expectations for all He has to teach us. As we take the time to be still and know that He is God, He gives us real rest. He stills these storms as only He can. He calls us by name.

REST

My friend Carol balances her active family commitments with the dynamic women's ministry she leads in a large church. In her insight, she notes:

> Rest isn't always a popular choice these days. It doesn't gain us likes or followers on social media. It is oftentimes seen as selfish or lazy. It goes against the world's narrative to be busy and to stay busy.
>
> But God never intended us to live apart from Him, meaning that He never intended us to become swallowed up in stress, busyness, or constant striving. All these things vie for our attention, distract our focus off of Him, and can sap our energy. That is why it is so important to take the time to sink into the healing and energizing rest that is found in Jesus. It is there that we receive restoration and peace, clarity and purpose. There, we can reflect, listen, or simply be. And in doing so, we are that much more equipped and prepared to tackle life's daily challenges.[79]

DISCUSSION QUESTION 3 How would you describe the world's narrative for busyness as opposed to rest? According to Carol's wise words, what impact can busyness have on us? What benefits of time with Jesus does she list?

LEARNING AT THE LORD'S FEET

Jesus had a way of turning a cultural norm on its ear, and this situation was no different! Mary's position at Jesus' feet was that of a student learning from a rabbi.[80] "In Jewish tradition, females were not normally allowed to study and become disciples of a rabbi. . . . Jesus defend[s] Mary for choosing to receive instruction."[81] In her book *The Heart of Jesus*, Marlys Taege Moberg wrote that Jesus' words concerning Mary still speak to us today, specifically to us as women. "[Jesus' answer] approves and encourages our study of Christ's message and mission. . . . He welcomed Mary as a full participant."[82] Jesus wants us to grow continually in His Word and in the knowledge of His will.

> **R&R:** How does Jesus' unique attitude toward women affect you? Talk about it.

THE GOOD PORTION

Make no mistake: Martha's service to the Lord and His disciples was good. Nevertheless, the portion Mary chose was even better. I love the word picture that Jesus gives us here. "The good portion" (verse 42) beautifully compares receiving God's Word to eating a meal. Food is consumed and gone, and hunger will come again, "but the Word of the Lord remains forever" (1 Peter 1:25), eternally satisfying a deeper hunger.[83] God's love revealed in His Word will settle any storm that you yourself have brewed up. Then your work won't be a burden but a service of joy.

Pastor Jonathon Krenz, in a recent *Portals of Prayer* devotion, spoke of "the good portion" so succinctly, I couldn't help but share:

> You are not saved by serving. You are saved by Jesus, who imparts His salvation to you in His Word. Go sit at His feet and rest in the Gospel. That is the good portion, and it will not be taken away from you. Then, having heard, get up and get to work. It's all good![84]

Jesus provides the refuge we need from our worries, scurries, and distractions. To be still before Him is to find rest for our lives and for our souls!

I'M SUCH A MARTHA

With an eye roll and a sigh, we say, "I'm such a Martha." Others, such as my friend Elizabeth, laugh and nod knowingly, because they can relate too. The catchphrase may even resonate with women who aren't familiar with the biblical text but know that *Martha* here means someone who can't sit still, a doer of many things! We may downplay it or laugh over it. We might even think we've earned a place in the Martha Club and a stressed-out, I'm-busier-than-you badge.

> **R&R:** Have you ever used the Martha catchphrase? If so, what was the context? Where else have you heard it?

Burning both ends of the proverbial candle means it burns twice as fact, right? When will it burn out completely? What does that look like for you? Maybe it means earlier mornings and later nights just so you can get it all done or fit it all in. Or maybe the threat of burnout comes from a failure to take care of your body and soul.

> **R&R:** On a scale of one to ten, with one being quietest and ten being craziest, mark where portions of your day fall:

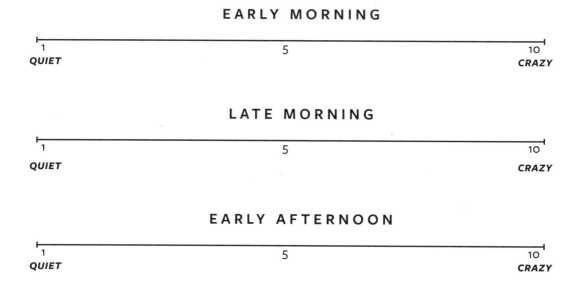

EARLY MORNING

1 — QUIET .... 5 .... 10 — CRAZY

LATE MORNING

1 — QUIET .... 5 .... 10 — CRAZY

EARLY AFTERNOON

1 — QUIET .... 5 .... 10 — CRAZY

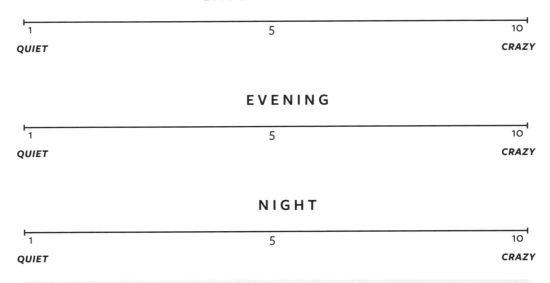

LATE AFTERNOON

1   5   10

QUIET   **CRAZY**

EVENING

1   5   10

QUIET   **CRAZY**

NIGHT

1   5   10

QUIET   **CRAZY**

R&R: Do you find yourself filling every waking moment with commitments, work, and activities so that you end up ignoring your need for rest, reflection, and a real refill? What part of your day could you commit to soul care? What solution would help you maintain the commitments that are most important?

Elizabeth found a solution that enabled her to have intentional time for soul care and still bless others by her hospitality. She let go of her desire to do "one more thing" so she could still open her home while achieving some semblance of balance and rest in a rigorous season of life. She shared:

> During a busy time in my life, I hosted a 5:30 p.m. weekly Bible study small group in my home. Though nothing was said about food the first week, I knew everyone would be hungry, and I threw together whatever was in my fridge. Each week became basically like that: we ate whatever was in my fridge or pantry (a snack, a salad, leftovers, or cheese and crackers). My guests were thrilled to have a bite to eat, and my focus remained on them.[85]

JOURNAL: What one takeaway today enables me to say, "I can be still because I know that He is God"?

DAY 4: WHAT'S MY MOTIVATION?

THREE RED FLAGS

Let's take a closer look at Martha's service and the motivation behind it. Three red flags stand out: (1) Control: Martha sought control of the situation, of Mary, and even of Jesus. (2) Comparison: By comparing her service to Mary's, Martha became critical of any service other than her own. (3) Self-service: Martha's self-focus is evident in her outburst of self-pity, which referred to "me" and "my" more than anyone else. Martha was using her gift of hospitality to serve the Lord, but neglecting "the good portion" was the demise of her service.

Now take a close look at your own service. Ask yourself, "What is my motivation behind it?" The same three red flags are a guarantee that your service will struggle.

> **R&R:** Following each question, I have provided my thoughts. Underline words that resonate with you as you reflect upon possible motivations behind your service. Provide additional thoughts as you wish.

1. **CONTROL:** Do you feel the need to control situations or people when you serve?

Too easily, I become defensive if the situation is not going the way I had planned, if people aren't cooperating as I expect, or if others don't follow my (sometimes implied) lead.

2. **COMPARISON:** Do you let your work define you? Do you compare your service with someone else's?

I admit that I have attempted to find my significance and my value in my service. But God says I am defined solely by my relationship with Him. He is the One who gives me value, just as He gives me talent, gifts, opportunities, and a purpose for the work I do. If it isn't rooted in Him, it may become a mere storm of scurry. Caught up in a storm of my own making, I am headed downhill, drenched by a downpour, traveling a slippery slope. The next thing I know, I'm using my service to compare myself to others, and comparing is rarely pretty. I am either disappointed or disillusioned.

3. **SELF-SERVICE:** Do you make your service all about you?

I have to ask myself: is my focus on my service and what I'm doing, rather than on the One I'm serving? Am I more concerned about appreciation, success, or recognition? When this happens, I need to recalibrate my focus and reexamine my motives and purpose. True service begins as an outpouring of His love in me: it's my response, out of love for Him and as shown through my service. Colossians 3:23–24 is a perfect reminder of who and how: "Whatever you do, work heartily, as for the Lord and not for men. . . . You are serving the Lord Christ."

Reevaluate your reasons for serving. If your motivation is anything less than love, confess it before the Lord, receive His forgiveness, and follow His lead (and not necessarily your agenda). Let your reasons reside with the One who is actually in control. Draw near to Him first. Receive "the good portion": sit at His feet. Let Him give you direction, desire, and strength to serve. Yes, service is important, but it is second to a loving relationship with the Lord; in fact, it's a natural outpouring of it. Relationship with the Lord enables an otherwise tiresome task to become a service of joy.

DISCUSSION QUESTION 1 Read 1 Corinthians 13:1–3. What one thing makes all the difference in what we do and how we serve? What are we without it?

All we do would be void of meaning without love. May the cry of our heart be "Lord, let all I do be done in love!"

MY TO-DO LIST

Can I confess to you that I find self-gratification in the completion of one item after another on my to-do list, even when that means I may scurry to make it happen? I may even add things to my list as they're completed, just so I have more to mark off! (Sheesh!) When I'm in this mode, watch out! Those who get in the way may get swept up in my storm. To be honest, I've fallen for this deception: accomplishing things makes me a good person; failing to accomplish things makes me a bad person. I devalue things that are difficult to measure or check off my list.

What does that mean regarding my daily walk with the Lord and time with Him? Does my devotion or Bible study time make my list? That would give it some space in my day, but it could easily become another check mark to my mile-long list—an obligation or a duty.

I'm a work in progress, and so are you. We've heard or said, "If I could just get a little peace and quiet!" This is precisely what the Lord provides: peace in His presence. He leads us to stop and bask in the quiet time that He provides in His Word so we may be still before Him and know that He is God. He is Lord and leader of our days. He will be exalted as we humble ourselves before Him, receiving what we need for the day. Read what He says to us in these verses:

I am with you.	Psalm 46:7, 11
I am for you.	Romans 8:31–32
I hear you.	Psalm 18:6
I have you in My grip.	Psalm 73:23
I love you.	Isaiah 43:4

DISCUSSION QUESTION 2 Look up each of the passages above and personalize them to your faith walk, as if God is speaking to you (because He is).

Sometimes my opportunities to be still before the Lord are highlighted by words from another believer who speaks into my situation. My friend Michelle does exactly that through her podcast, *Peace in His Presence*. Imagine how my jaw dropped as I heard a recent episode and Michelle shared a powerful way to pray through our theme verse for this study.[86] I've added verse references to include a bit of Scripture study with it:

> **R&R:** Meditate on Psalm 46:10, focusing on the word in italics. Pause to read each corresponding verse and consider the depth of meaning in each one. Take it to the Lord in prayer and praise.

"Be still, and know that I am *God*." Read Ephesians 1:17.

"Be still, and know that *I am*." Read Exodus 3:14; John 14:6.

"Be still, and *know*." Read John 8:32.

"Be *still*." Read Psalm 23:2.

"*Be*." Read Psalm 37:7a.

JOURNAL: What one takeaway today enables me to say, "I can be still because I know that He is God"?

DAY 5: GENTLE REDIRECTION

GOD'S WORD

My friend Michelle spoke right to my heart in her podcast. She said:

> Being still before the Lord doesn't mean that your thoughts quiet down or that your circumstances quiet down. Or that anything necessarily changes. It means sitting with God in whatever capacity you are . . . whether you are an anxious hot mess or feeling pretty good. Bring everything to God and hand it all over to Him; He brings you His peace. Let God be God. You get to be His child.[87]

Through the Spirit's leading, we long to sit at our Savior's feet as Mary did, hanging on to His every word. We can sit at His feet today, with His Word before us and His Spirit within us. He teaches, and we learn (without employing a single to-do list). The Spirit enables our understanding and further strengthens our faith.

Your desire to sit at Jesus' feet says much about your heart and your acknowledgment of your need. It may stem from past times of devotion, when time with Him made a difference in your day and further impacted your heart. Now you yearn for more, continually more aware of His love for you as you are led by His Word.

> **R&R:** How can sitting at Jesus' feet provide refuge for you and make the self-inflicted storms of scurry subside? Why is time in God's Word vital to your spiritual health?

God's Word empowers us by the Spirit, reminding us that He is present. He is our strength and our help in trouble; He is our help when *we* are troubled. Storms of our own making will subside as He changes our heart, our focus, and our attitude. We can give Jesus the stressors that cause emotional and mental storms in our lives: our expectations of ourselves and of others; our agitations with those closest to us; the many things that worry, trouble, and distract us. Jesus does not want us swept away by storms of scurry any more than He wants us to be blown over by the storms caused by sin, which He removed by His death on the cross. He is our refuge in every storm.

God's Word reveals Jesus' work. He cleanses our souls, creates faith, and continues His good work in us. Isaiah 55:11 contains God's promise: "So shall My word be that goes out from My mouth; it shall not return to Me empty, but it shall accomplish that which I purpose, and shall succeed in the thing for which I sent it."

FIRST PRIORITY

Jesus spoke the truth in love to Martha, gently guiding her to reevaluate her priorities. He not only supported her but also helped her see the bigger picture more clearly. Martha sought to do her best for Jesus, but Jesus knew what was truly best for Martha. Gently, He led her to it, through His words and by His grace. She knew Jesus loved her, so she could trust His guidance.

DISCUSSION QUESTION 1 Read Ephesians 4:15. Who has spoken the truth in love to you after you've allowed yourself to be blown about in a storm of scurry? What made it possible or effective for them to do so?

Martha was not always in a storm of scurry, as she was here. Martha's faith was strong. Her trust in Jesus' healing power and her profession of faith in Him, even at her brother's death, was steadfast and unswerving (John 11:21–27). She knew His love, and she grew in love. Jesus returned to dine in Martha's home, after His miracle at Lazarus's tomb. Their family held a special meal in honor of their Lord, who had conquered death. Jesus reclined again at the table. Lazarus and others were there too. Mary was again at Jesus' feet, this time anointing them with perfume. And Martha was serving again, as she did so well. This time, however, we read nothing of anxiety or agitation, just straightforward service out of love for her Lord (John 12:1–8).

DISCUSSION QUESTION 2 Based on what we read in John 11–12, how do you think Martha responded to Jesus' words of redirection in the account in Luke 10? What impact did Jesus' words have on her?

The Lord leads us to His Word, and we grow in love, trust, knowledge, and faith. Service is our natural response.

> **R&R:** Look for where and how the Lord is moving, and join Him on His mission. All that you do in your vocations is His work, so ask Him: how would He have you serve today? Where will you be used by Him?

Yes, our dear Martha, in her self-inflicted storm of scurry, sought help from Jesus to straighten out her sister. She received, instead, exactly what she needed: gentle truth from the Savior. She found refuge in His response to her, as He taught her to rest in His presence. He lovingly redirected her away from the storm of her own making. She could be still at His feet and know that He is God.

We, too, can be still before the Lord: we acknowledge Him as Lord of the universe and Lord of our lives, our refuge and our strength. We don't need to fret or fear, because He is our help in every trouble and our help when *we* are troubled. All-powerful, always-present, and exalted, He is the one in charge. We seek Him first and sit at His feet.

"BE STILL!"

I would say I came into the world with the gift of gab, though I'm not sure my teachers or parents always saw it as a gift. In the classroom, at the dinner table, and in any number of other settings, I was told to "be still." Stop talking for a bit. Breathe. Eat. Rest. Do my schoolwork. Let someone else talk. I didn't have a problem sitting; I just couldn't be silent. It took time, practice, and God's help to learn to be still—quiet and restful—before the Lord. I have to remind myself to create space in my days to just be, to listen as He speaks to me.

In His mighty power, the Holy Spirit quiets us with His presence, calms us with His comfort, and draws us toward Himself that we may "be still, and know" (Psalm 46:10). It is during those times of stillness when we stop to pray, when we sit quietly in God's Word, that we are reminded again that He is God. He alone has control of all things. He is all-powerful and almighty, defeating sin, death, and the devil at the cross and the empty tomb. By His power at work in us, Christ will be exalted in our lives, both today and as we await His return at the final resurrection!

> **R&R:** "God is our refuge and strength, a very present help in trouble" (Psalm 46:1). In light of all you've learned in this session, in what ways can you say that Jesus fulfills these words of the psalmist for you? What does your Refuge's gift of *rest* mean to you? How does He daily provide gentle *redirection*? What might your response be?

JOURNAL: What one takeaway today enables me to say, "I can be still because I know that He is God"?

VIEWER GUIDE

SESSION 5: STORMS OF SCURRY

Sometimes, surrender means _____ our days, _____ our priorities, or _____ those things that distract us or keep us from the one thing that matters most.

Turn to Luke 10:38–42.

In a flurried storm of scurry, Martha asked for assistance but received, instead, the opportunity to _____, to find respite in Him, along with gentle _____ to sit first at His feet.

To be still is challenging, since our storms of scurry involve our whole self—body, mind, heart, and soul.

• To _____ be still is to stop, and to calm our flurry of activity.

• To _____ be still is to calm our swirling thoughts, take them captive, and make them obedient to Christ (2 Corinthians 10:5).

• To _____ be still is to calm our anxious heart, our chaotic emotions.

• Above all, we can _____ be still because we know that He is God, our Savior. We can stop. Let go. Be still before the Lord, and take everything to Him in prayer.

Jesus, the one thing necessary, provides His gifts:

• Redemption, _____, and _____, along with a refill.

• _____ in faith, understanding, and insight.

• _____ for purpose and _____ for service.

DISCUSS

> God is our refuge and strength, a very present help in trouble. Therefore we will not fear though the earth gives way, though the mountains be moved into the heart of the sea, though its waters roar and foam, though the mountains tremble at its swelling. . . . "Be still, and know that I am God." (Psalm 46:1–3, 10)

As you consider your storms of scurry, what do your roaring waters and trembling mountains look like? How is your storm brewing or blowing in a specific situation? What trouble has come because of this storm?

Can you see God working to calm you or calm the storm, helping you to trust Him in it? How do you know that He is God and R.E.S.T. (*refuge, ever*-present *strength* in *trouble*) in that truth? How or where do you see His help?

READY TO R.E.S.T.?

READ AND REFLECT: What do the Scriptures and this Bible study say about storms of scurry? What do they say about Jesus, your refuge in this storm? What were your biggest takeaways?

EXAMINE QUESTIONS AND EXPLORE ANSWERS: For greater understanding and for application, seek answers in Scripture and meditate upon the personal questions.

SHARE: Tell about your takeaways and your storm, with a group or alone, as you write or pray about them.

TRUST your Refuge, the One who provides *rest* and *redirection*.

STORMS OF SADNESS

MARTHA AND MARY—JOHN 11:1-44

DAY 1: "ARE YOU THERE, LORD?"

FROM THE HEART

I recently attended a Sidewalk Prophets concert on a Christian college campus, thanks to my friends Kris and Elli. They even secured after-concert passes, and a small group of us enjoyed a candy buffet, games, and conversation with the four-person band. Hearing the band members speak from their hearts, I knew I wanted to keep up with them. Prior to a new release, "Real to Me," they explained their vulnerable thoughts and prayers that led them to the lyrics, and they allowed me to share them here with you:

> "Are you there?" That is the question that haunts so many of us. Sometimes, in our hour of desperation, we cry out. We cry out to hear your voice, we plead to see your face, and we pray to understand. Many times, in fact, most times, our ears are deaf to hear your voice, and our eyes are blind to see your ways.

> Hopelessness, fearfulness, [sadness], and confusion are the emotions that twist our souls into knots. We are held captive by our doubts and pinned down by our expectations. Some people talk about the light at the end of the tunnel. Others talk about calm after the storm, but none of that seems to matter when we're bogged down in the marshes of it. We are grasping for safety and security wherever an opportunity presents itself.

> Why does faith come so easily for others? How can they find joy so readily in all the adversity? Where is the joy in uncertainty? Where is the peace when it feels like death's walls are closing in on us?[88]

Let's pause here. You will hear a happier ending to this prayer from Sidewalk Prophets, but let's examine some of these thoughts for ourselves. Let's hear from two sisters who experienced similar feelings of fear, sadness, and doubt.

Maybe you haven't said these words aloud, but you've thought something similar. "Are You there, God? You didn't fix things like I thought You would." You've cried out in desperation; you have pleaded to see His face. Maybe, like the band, you were once pinned down with expectations, and when they didn't happen, you struggled with doubt. Your faith has been put to the test. In the storm, maybe you've grasped for security and sought refuge in something else, but to no avail.

R&R: Does God appear to be distant or even unavailable sometimes? When you don't receive the solution that you sought or a recognizable answer to your cry, does it mean He isn't listening? Is it okay to admit your doubts and fears? Can you acknowledge your sadness, even hopelessness?

R&R: Has it ever seemed to you that God is slow to answer? "Lord, if only You had . . ." Recall a time and share. What was (or was not) happening that led you to feel this way?

TWO SISTERS' STORM OF SADNESS—BASED ON JOHN 11:1–44

Lazarus was gravely ill. Martha and Mary feared the worst, but they knew the concern Jesus would have for their brother because they knew His love. When they sent word of his sickness to Jesus, they simply said, "Lord, he whom You love is ill" (John 11:3). Jesus would know. Martha and Mary trusted that He would come to heal their brother. They knew He could. Surely, He would hurry. So they waited, watching as Lazarus's health failed. But Jesus had not come. Grief saturated their hearts. The funeral and burial followed. Mourners arrived for the customary seven-day period of grieving. Friends provided comfort, but the One from whom they sought it most still had not arrived. The days crept by.

Finally, on the fourth day after Lazarus's death, Martha spotted Jesus coming up the road. While Mary and many of the other mourners remained at their home, Martha ran out to meet Him and cried out, "Lord, if You had been here, my brother would not have died" (verse 21). Words tumbled from the lips of a woman with a broken heart, swept up in a storm of sadness. She wasn't angry, just deeply distressed and sorrowful. She had been certain of Jesus' love; if only He had been there to heal. But now it was much too late.

Martha continued, revealing her belief in Jesus' power, wisdom, and obedience to the Father: "Even now I know that whatever You ask from God, God will give You" (verse 22). When Jesus replied, "Your brother will rise again" (verse 23), Martha nodded. "I know that He will rise again in the resurrection on the last day" (verse 24), she replied, thinking Jesus meant the final resurrection. She knew and believed God's resurrection promise to His people.

What Jesus said next, though, flooded her with unspeakable joy: "I am the resurrection and the life. Whoever believes in Me, though he die, yet shall he live, and everyone who lives and believes in Me shall never die" (verses 25–26). His words affirmed her greatest hope: all who believe in Him, though they die physically, will be raised to life forever!

Jesus continued with compassion, "Do you believe this?" (verse 26).

Martha exclaimed, "Yes, Lord; I believe that You are the Christ, the Son of God" (verse 27).

Martha ran back to the house to tell Mary that the Teacher had come. No sooner had she spoken than Mary rose and ran to Jesus too, with the mourners right behind her. Mary fell at Jesus' feet in tears, blurting the same sad words of her sister, "Lord, if You had been here, my brother would not have died" (verse 32).

Jesus looked down at her face, then at the tears of the mourners. He was deeply moved. "Where have you laid him?" He asked (verse 34). They led Him to the tomb, and Jesus wept. He wept out of love for Martha and Mary and for all who mourned. He wept because He felt the pain His people were suffering; their pain was His pain; their grief was His grief. "See how He loved him!" some said (verse 36).

A stone covered the cave's opening, where Lazarus's body had been lain. When Jesus commanded the stone be taken away, Martha gasped. What was He doing? Hastily, she warned Him of the odor emitted by a body that had been buried for four days. Jesus said to her, "Did I not tell you that if you believed you would see the glory of God?" (verse 40). The stone was taken away, and Jesus lifted His face to the Father, praying aloud for the sake of all who would hear, so that they might believe. "Father, I thank You that You have heard Me. I knew that You always hear Me, but I said this on account of the people standing around, that they may believe that You sent Me" (verses 41–42).

Martha and Mary could hardly believe their ears when Jesus cried out loudly, "Lazarus, come out" (verse 44). Their brother, four days dead, appeared before them, alive and well. God the Son raised Lazarus from the dead. He who is the resurrection and the life revealed His power over the grave and His victory over sin. There was great rejoicing that day!

> **R&R:** Ponder the story of Martha and Mary's storm of sadness (read John 11:1–44). Then write what stood out to you. What was your first and immediate takeaway? Revisit the message from Sidewalk Prophets now, in light of the sisters' story. How do the two compare?

DISCUSSION QUESTION 1 "God is our refuge and strength, a very present help in trouble" (Psalm 46:1). In what ways did Jesus fulfill these words of the psalmist for Martha and Mary? How was He their refuge in their storm?

In their storm of sadness, Martha and Mary asked for their brother's healing but received, instead, his *resurrection*, along with the *reassurance* of the final *resurrection* for all who believe.

DISCUSSION QUESTION 2 "Be still, and know that I am God. I will be exalted among the nations, I will be exalted in the earth!" (Psalm 46:10). Picture the lives of Martha and Mary after their encounter with Christ. How do you think these words would have spoken to them? How was Jesus exalted in their lives and in the world?

FROM THE HEART, CONTINUED:

When we've given up hope; when we're broken, helpless, and defeated, that is when it happens. You've never been more real than in this moment. If we hide the fact that we ever doubted, then those with doubts wouldn't feel like somebody knows what they're dealing with. So instead, we choose to sing about and celebrate the questions, the trials, the miles, and the days of doubt and fear because they truly are the things that make us who we are. They are the things that got us here. So, "Hallelujah for the questions and trials. Hallelujah for the road and all the miles. Hallelujah for the days of doubt and fear. Hallelujah for the things that got us here."[89]

—**Sidewalk Prophets**

143

We read in the Epistle of James:

> Count it all joy, my brothers, when you meet trials of various kinds, for you know that the testing of your faith produces steadfastness. And let steadfastness have its full effect, that you may be perfect and complete, lacking in nothing. (James 1:2–4)

R&R: Can God work through your brokenness and your feelings of doubt and defeat? Absolutely! Take another peek at James 1:2–4. Have you considered who may benefit when you share your vulnerable feelings, your doubts, sadness, and fear? He meets you where you are, weeps with you, and reveals that He is as real as He is victorious, now and in the final resurrection. Alleluia!

He is with you. He is your Refuge and your Strength. He says, "Be still, and know that I am God" (Psalm 46:10). He is incomparably greater than any storm of sadness that threatens to sweep you away.

JOURNAL: What one takeaway today enables me to say, "I can be still because I know that He is God"?

DAY 2: JESUS LOVES YOU

THE ONE YOU LOVE

"Back door guests are best," the sign in the store said. That could be tricky, I thought. What if I'm the type of guest who only uses the front door? Would that make me less than the best? Then I smiled to myself as I thought more about the point of the message. What a privilege it is to be the neighbor or friend who feels comfortable coming in the back way, in view of rooms not necessarily kept tidy for company. If Mary, Martha, and Lazarus had a back door to their home, Jesus would have walked right through it. They were *that* close. How sweet it is to enjoy fellowship with people who make you feel at home, who provide rest and respite, who treat you like family.

This family of three siblings was close to Jesus and His disciples, who reclined and dined in their Bethany home on more than a few occasions. When the sisters sent word to Jesus, they spoke confidently of His love for Lazarus, the brotherly love (Greek *phileo*) of a friend.[90] The message did not say, "Come!" Rather, it said, "He whom You love is ill" (John 11:3). They may have contacted other friends with this same news, but Jesus was their beloved Teacher, Brother, and Friend. They had witnessed His miraculous work. They believed in Him and His power.

Don't miss the significance of the sisters' description of their brother. What identified Lazarus? It was Jesus' love for him, yes, but an even greater love than the one of which they spoke. As John penned this Gospel by the inspiration of the Spirit, he wanted readers to be assured of Jesus' love for this family: "Now Jesus loved Martha and her sister and Lazarus" (John 11:5). John wrote of the unconditional love (Greek *agape*) of God, who fully "understands those loved, cares for them, and acts in their favor."[91] His *agape* was far greater than the *phileo*, of which they were certain.

You are known and loved too. Your loved ones could cry to Jesus on your behalf and simply say, "The one You love, Lord." Like Martha, Mary, and Lazarus, you love the Lord—but far greater is His love for you, perhaps more than you realize. "In this is love, not that we have loved God but that He loved us and sent His Son" (1 John 4:10).

> R&R: What identifies you? "Jesus love[s] _____." (Insert your name in place of those in John 11:5.) Confident of His love, you can send word to Him, sharing your problems and your pain. What can you do if no word returns or comes when you expect it?

DISCUSSION QUESTION 1 God is love, and you are the object of His love. God demonstrated it, countless verses proclaim it, and you are defined by it. Receive affirmation of His love for you in this small sampling of verses, all from one New Testament book: 1 John 3:1; 3:16; 4:9; 4:16; 4:19. Name something specific about God's love for you from each verse.

PERFECT TIMING?

Jesus assured His disciples that Lazarus's "illness does not lead to death" (John 11:4). But wait a minute—it had lead to death! What could Jesus have meant?

Jesus' delay was seemingly neglectful, but it was actually quite the opposite. With deliberate timing and steps, in obedience to God's plan, Jesus stayed away from Bethany during a critical time. Jesus' always-perfect timing allowed Him to restore Lazarus, who was "four days dead, when corruption has set in, . . . when all human experience cries out, 'Too late!' when faith can be only faith in the God 'who gives life to the dead and calls into existence the things that do not exist' (Romans 4:17)."[92]

According to rabbinic belief, the soul hovered over the body of the deceased for three days and then departed when decomposition set in. "Only a genuine miracle could account for the raising of Lazarus."[93] Only God could perform such a miracle. Jesus' perfect timing enabled many people to witness Him raising Lazarus, and word spread like wildfire (see John 12:17). Who could then deny that Jesus was the Son of God in the flesh, the promised Messiah? If the religious leaders had felt threatened before, this miracle would be the act that set in motion the plot for Jesus' crucifixion—God's salvation plan from the beginning. Jesus had "set His face to go to Jerusalem" (Luke 9:51). His time had come. Of course, Martha and Mary didn't know this; they had simply sent word to the One they knew could heal. The timing of His arrival didn't appear perfect to them—not yet, anyway.

Still, Martha's faith was evident. She knew Jesus could have prevented death. She believed Jesus would have healed her brother, had He been present. Can you imagine the questions (and even doubts) she and Mary may have asked each other, in addition to the one she blurted to Jesus as soon as she saw Him? "Didn't He know that time was short? Why hadn't He arrived already? He had healed so many others; why not Lazarus, the one whom He loved?"

WORKING WHILE WE WAIT

Recalling this account in her Bible study *Waiting*, author Sharla Fritz said, "God loves us enough to want us to grow in trust. He is more concerned about our faith than our temporary comfort."[94] We can trust that He is working while we are waiting—for help, for an answer, for comfort that hasn't yet come. Waiting "may not only be for the sake of our faith, but for the faith of those who watch us patiently endure."[95]

We may reason that our faith would surely be stronger if we didn't have to wait, if we didn't feel discomfort. But growth is most evident in our trial and as we wait.

> **R&R:** Recall a time of waiting. When have you witnessed a person of faith patiently wait and endure? What kind of impact did it have on you?

I BELIEVE!

We have been in Martha's situation. Even if we haven't suffered the death of a dear loved one, we've still endured deep loss: the end of a relationship, family dysfunction, healing that doesn't come, the death of a dream, and so on. Though we find ourselves in the depths of sadness over our situations, our faith remains strong because we believe that Jesus is the Son of God and our Savior. Even when our questions go unanswered, by God's grace, we can cling to the faith we profess: Jesus is Lord. He is the resurrection. He is life.

Even in Martha's grief, she made a profound profession of faith in the final resurrection for all who believe. Martha confidently confessed that Lazarus would rise on the Last Day. In turn, Jesus assured Martha concerning all who believe in Him, that though they die physically, they will live forever. They will physically rise to eternal life in a bodily resurrection. "Physical death is no obstacle to the resurrection."[96]

"Do you believe this?" Because of her faith, Martha could say "I believe!" May our answer, like Martha's, be the cry of our heart: "Yes! I believe!"

DISCUSSION QUESTION 2 What is especially significant about the order of events, including Martha's confession and Lazarus's resurrection? What does that say about Martha's faith?

DISCUSSION QUESTION 3 As you read the verses below, ponder the words of the psalmist. How do they relate to Martha's immediate response to Jesus' arrival and to her display of faith that followed? What similarities do you see? How can you personalize these verses when you're struggling in a storm?

> On God rests my salvation and my glory; my mighty rock, my refuge is God. Trust in Him at all times, O people; pour out your heart before Him; God is a refuge for us. (Psalm 62:7–8)

Following Martha's great statement of faith, she let Mary know that Jesus had come. Mary "rose quickly" (John 11:29)—she ran to Jesus and fell at His feet. The first words to tumble from her lips were a repeat of Martha's: "Lord, if You had been here, my brother would not have died" (verse 32). Throughout the long days of waiting and weeping, looking and longing for Jesus' arrival, the sisters must have repeated this to each other. Though they doubted because of Jesus' seeming delay, Mary expressed the same faith as her sister: she, too, was certain of Jesus' healing power. She needed the consolation of the Teacher, at whose feet she had sat before.

R&R: We can imagine the incredible impact of Jesus' teachings on both Mary and Martha, enabling them to be so certain of His healing power. When has His Word provided consolation for you? How can you know for certain that Jesus is working through His Word to impact you today? See 1 Thessalonians 2:13.

JOURNAL: What one takeaway today enables me to say, "I can be still because I know that He is God"?

DAY 3: HE KNOWS YOUR PAIN

WE ESCAPED!

My family found a new pastime not too long ago: escape rooms. When our kids were home for Christmas, we solved a mystery in a medieval castle—we secured the keys and made our escape. Of course, we weren't locked inside a real castle, but we unraveled a mystery, cracked every code, and won the game. Following our escape, we posed for a picture, each holding a silly sign that spoke of our success. My husband's sign read simply, "We escaped!"

The getaway with our kids felt like a temporary escape from the realities of life, from the difficulties of the previous weeks. In the months prior, we had wept beside loved ones and prayed with others countless times. We'd walked beside people of our community during devastating pain and loss: widespread flood damage, cancer diagnoses, family breakdown, and deaths.

No one escapes storms, whether they are natural disasters, health crises, relationship strains, or losses of life. But we do not weep alone. The Lord knows and feels our pain. He is our refuge—a strong tower (incomparably stronger than any castle). He is our strength when we are weak and weepy. He is our help in every trial and trouble.

No matter what we face, you and I and all believers in Christ can cling to this truth: we escaped. We escaped from bondage to freedom and from death to life, but not by our own doing. His death is the only key that could unlock us from the chains of sin by which we were bound. He secured our salvation. He allowed Himself to be captured so we could escape.

JESUS WEPT

Two words. The shortest verse in the Bible is also one of the most profound. He "shed tears" quietly (Greek *dakryo*), not in loud lamentation (Greek *klaio*).[97] In this verse, we see the heart of our Savior and Lord. Jesus felt the grief the sisters were suffering. When Jesus arrived to find His friends mourning, He was moved to tears out of love for them.[98] Though He knew He would raise Lazarus from the sleep of death, He broke down and wept too.

When Jesus experienced sadness, He dealt with it a few different ways. Sometimes He went away to be alone with God. He prayed. He moved toward others, out of compassion for them. And He wept.

Jesus mourns over sin and its awful effects. He hates death, the cruel and sad result of sin. When His people are saddened with suffering, He is too. If you've ever wondered if Jesus knows your heart, return to this passage and recall that He wept. Even the certain hope of the resurrection did not keep Him from crying for His friends.

DISCUSSION QUESTION 1 When else did Jesus weep? A few passages provide us a glimpse. Read Luke 19:41–42; Hebrews 5:7; John 11:35. What was the context, the reason He wept?

DISCUSSION QUESTION 2 Does it comfort you to know that Jesus wept for His people then? He knows and feels your pain now too. Read Isaiah 53:4 and write the first half of the verse here: _____. What word makes Isaiah's prophesy of Jesus especially personal? Whose griefs, sorrows, and pain did Jesus bear? What did Jesus do with them?

Jesus knows our hearts, hears our cries, and sees our tears. His compassion is so great, His knowledge so intimate; He carries our sorrows. Rest in this truth when you grow impatient waiting for an answer or when you grow concerned, wondering if He knows or cares. He does—more than we can comprehend this side of heaven. When sadness penetrates your heart, believe that He hurts for you and with you.

The storms of sadness will hit, and some with great ferocity. Let the tears flood like rain, washing over you and bearing testimony to the depth of your love, your grief, and your loss. "Sadness does not mean you're without hope. . . . Your sadness honors your love, your hopes, your dreams, and your relationships. . . . Tears will not hold you captive in sadness; they will free you for a future of joy and gladness."[99]

> **R&R:** Your tears bear testimony to so much. Though your storm may or may not produce a steady stream of tears, when have your tears felt cathartic? When have tears been beneficial, even therapeutic?

He sees you in this storm. Your sadness matters to God because you are precious to Him. He knows the intricate details of your life and what produces the emotional pain you bear. Acknowledge it to Him. Shed tears. He does.

SOMETHING GREATER

Jesus was the refuge for Martha and Mary in their storm of sadness as they faced death. It was the lack of Jesus' presence (or so Martha and Mary thought) that kept their brother from receiving the healing for which they'd hoped. But the timing for Jesus' presence in their midst provided greater healing, a greater purpose.

> **R&R:** In your storms of sadness, when have you been able to recognize His fortress of protection as your refuge? How have you noticed His presence, receiving reminders that He is with you? Where have you seen His help in your trouble?

> **R&R:** Have you considered that Jesus' seeming delay to your cry in the storm might mean He is doing something greater that you simply cannot see yet? Could it be that His answer may arrive in a way that is currently unrecognizable to you?

Like Martha and Mary, we can be honest in our cries to the Lord.

DISCUSSION QUESTION 3 Compare Jesus' responses to Martha (John 11:23, 25–26) to His answer to Mary (John 11:33–35). How and why were they different? What do we learn about Jesus' heart as we look at both?

Jesus comes to us, hears us, and receives us as we are. Do we need comfort, empathy, answers? Do we need words that remind us of our faith? He knows, and He provides all we need through His Word, through the peace He instills through prayer, and through fellow people of faith.

JOURNAL: What one takeaway today enables me to say, "I can be still because I know that He is God"?

DAY 4: THE RESURRECTION AND THE LIFE

LIFESAVER

No one escapes some sadness in this life, but we are not without help when we face it. When you experience sadness, how do you deal with it? You could sink beneath the wild waves of despair, or you could reach out for the Lifesaver who's already in the water with you. The truth is that the Lifesaver encircles you already. Rest for a bit and let Him buoy you to a place of comfort. Trust the One who has you in His grip. Spend time in His Word and in prayer. Then, recognize that the same Lifesaver uses your friends of faith to buoy you in fellowship and hold you in prayer.

Maybe you just want to batten down the hatches so nothing—not the rain of the storm or the rays of the sun—can get in. Yes, you could let your sadness make you bitter. Or you can lean into the One who makes you better.

JESUS' PRAYER

> Father, I thank You that You have heard Me. I knew that You always hear Me, but I said this on account of the people standing around, that they may believe that You sent Me. (John 11:41–42)

Jesus knew the Father's plan and didn't have to pray aloud. He did so for the benefit of all who were witnesses: for all who would hear Him, then and now. He looked up to the Father above, pulling heavenward the attention of those who were watching. He thanked God for raising Lazarus before it even took place! "He was so in tune with the Father's will that He knew what the result would be. He wanted the Jews to hear Him call God His Father and believe that He was the Son of God, the Messiah sent from the Father."[100] Witnessing the miracle, all who were present would know His claims were true.

> **R&R:** What a wonder: God the Father gave His people the resurrection and the life in Jesus. God the Son intercedes for you, praying to the Father on your behalf and for your benefit (Hebrews 7:25). Praise Him now, lifting your hands and your voice to the Lord who is the resurrection and the life.

"LAZARUS, COME OUT" (JOHN 11:43)

Jesus called Lazarus by name, and immediately, he was awakened from death. Author Jane Fryar said it well:

> One day Jesus will speak our names too, and we will rise from the dust of death. It won't matter how long we've been dead. It won't matter whether our bodies are in a grave or lost at sea or scattered as ashes to the four winds. Jesus will speak, and our bodies will at that instant be reunited with our souls.[101]

There will be a great, never-ending celebration in the place of no tears, no mourning, no pain, and no death. We will celebrate His victory that's ours because of His amazing love. It is going to be the greatest homecoming party of all time! When you hear your name today, let it remind you that there will be a day when you will hear Jesus call your name and welcome you home.

As Jesus told His disciples, "This illness does not lead to death. It is for the glory of God, so that the Son of God may be glorified through it" (John 11:4). This miracle would display God's glory, and the Son would be glorified. God alone can raise the dead to life! Here, "glory" (Greek *doxa*) means "honor, glory, praise, and worship."[102] "Glorified" (Greek *doxazo*) means "to honor and to render glorious; to magnify."[103] When we magnify something, we see it more clearly. It's bigger and even more obvious to us.

This miracle "is the climax of the signs done by Jesus ([John] 20:30) the Man who loves, . . . who is deeply moved in spirit and troubled, . . . who weeps and prays."[104] God orchestrated these events so that people would praise Him and see Him more clearly. Through Lazarus's death and Jesus' resurrecting work, the Lord was magnified.

As Martha professed her faith; as Jesus proclaimed that He is the resurrection and the life; as Martha confessed, "I believe" (John 11:27)—in everything, Jesus was and is glorified!

R&R: Could a situation that has brought you much sadness actually bring glory to God? How may your circumstances magnify Him in your life as He carries you through them?

LIFE OVER DEATH

He may provide a miracle for you, but even if He doesn't, He still loves you. He calls you to praise Him! You can magnify Him as Martha did. You can trust Jesus' words in your storm: "This illness [or this time of sadness or suffering] does not [end in] death" (verse 4). Death is not the end. The ultimate comfort we can receive is this: even as we face the saddest of situations, even death, we who believe in Christ have certainty of our own resurrection to eternal life. For believers, death is a temporary interruption of the never-ending fellowship we have with one another.

DISCUSSION QUESTION 1 Jesus is life, just as He gives life to every believer. Death can never triumph! Read 1 Corinthians 15:54–57. What words define the life we have in Jesus? What happens to death?

When Lazarus was raised, God's purpose was twofold: He was glorified, and faith was furthered. Even before the miracle itself, Jesus told His disciples that through it, their faith would grow (see verses 14–15). Jesus demonstrated His power over the grave mere days before His own crucifixion and death, affirming His promise of eternal life and His divinity.

DISCUSSION QUESTION 2 Imagine the impact of this miracle on Jesus' disciples, on Martha and Mary, and on others who witnessed it. Read John 12:1–18, focusing on verses 1–2, 9–11, 17–18. What impact did the miracle have?

DISCUSSION QUESTION 3 Note the absolute contrast of "death" or "dead" and "life" in each of these verses. What brings death and what gives life? Make notes beside each reference.

Romans 5:21

Romans 6:23

Romans 8:2, 11

2 Timothy 1:10

See other sharp contrasts in Psalm 30:5, 11. What are they? How do they relate to the others above?

DISCUSSION QUESTION 4 "I am the resurrection and the life" (John 11:25). Read this sampling of several more verses in the Gospel of John, and summarize what you learn about eternal life and the only way to it. Write a word or phrase beside each reference that is unique to each verse.

John 1:4

John 6:40

John 10:10

John 14:6

John 20:31

JOURNAL: What one takeaway today enables me to say, "I can be still because I know that He is God"?

DAY 5: REASSURANCE OF HOPE AND JOY

I HAVE HOPE, BUT JOY?

So much sadness swept over our nation and our world as we faced the front end of the global Coronavirus pandemic. Only a few months later, acts of violence, murder, and hate roared with tidal-wave force across our country—more reminders of the sin-drenched world in which we live. As COVID-19 continued, we wondered when we would see loved ones again; what work would look like, following furloughs and closings; how life would appear when the viral storm had passed. We all knew people who were afflicted with and even died from the disease. Many things tested our faith and threatened our hope as we were bombarded by sad news day after day.

Then, as now and always, we look to God's Word for help and reassurance: "Rejoice in hope, be patient in tribulation, be constant in prayer" (Romans 12:12). Maybe you're thinking, "Wait a minute. Hope is one thing, but I'm supposed to be joyful too? Sounds like a stretch." Maybe joy seems out of reach—elusive. You don't have to slap on a happy face and fake how you feel.

In *Hope When Your Heart Breaks*, Pastor Michael Newman assures us:

> Jesus, your Savior, brings you the surprising prospect of joy through His life, death, and resurrection. . . . You don't have to be happy right now or try to forget your grief. Patience and perseverance are prerequisites. . . . At the right time, sooner or later, now or in eternity, your sadness will slip away.[105]

Are you still a person of joy, even in sadness? Absolutely! Expect Jesus to infuse some joy into your days, even—maybe especially—when you are feeling not one bit joyful.

Mindful of the words from Romans 12:12, and by God's grace, we can be faithful in prayer and patient in every affliction. Yes, we have certain hope in our Savior. But can we be joyful?

When we fix our focus on the storm around us, we easily lose heart and fail to find joy. What do we do then? We turn to God's Word.

DISCUSSION QUESTION 1 Turn to 2 Corinthians 4:18. We can fix our focus in either of two directions. What are our choices? How are they contrasted? How can we find comfort in this contrast?

> **R&R:** "The things that are seen" are evidence of our fallen, sinful world; they are temporary and fleeting. Look up 2 Corinthians 5:7, and write it here:

We look away from the fleeting things of this world and into the face of Jesus. He is at work through His Word and in the Sacraments. We see the fruits of faith evident in other believers too. We cling to God's promises, such as those found in James 1.

DISCUSSION QUESTION 2 Complete James 1:2–4 with key words: "Count it all _____, my brothers, when you meet _____ of various kinds, for you know that the testing of your _____ produces _____. And let _____ have its full effect, that you may be perfect and complete, lacking in _____."

"Count it all joy." Wait, what? Sure, we can swim through storms with hope and trust. But joy? Then we see why. The testing of our faith gives us perseverance: it makes us steadfast. We trust our Lord to use these storms for our growth and maturity in the faith, that we may, as James says, lack nothing. May we be able to pray, "Thank You, God, for allowing this storm. Use it to strengthen me. I have hope in Jesus; therefore, I can count it all joy too. In Jesus' name, I pray. Amen."

My friend Molly recently told me:

> I have a friend who expresses, "The joy of the Lord is [my] strength" often (Nehemiah 8:10). It's her life verse. I have watched her go through unspeakably difficult trials in this world, yet she proclaims God and brings glory to Him, even in the midst of despair and struggle. She also remembers to praise Him in the times of abundance and happiness. No matter what, all glory goes to God. I'm so glad she has set this example for me. I praise God for her.[106]

Count it all joy, indeed.

FILLING OR FEELINGS?

Still in need of reassurance? Turn to Psalm 42:5: "Why are you cast down, O my soul, and why are you in turmoil within me?" Sometimes we are overwhelmed or even surprised by sadness. Do you wonder, when you're at your saddest, if you will ever feel happy again? Maybe you're feeling *hurt, empty,* or even *hopeless.* Sometimes a situation or a relationship or life itself feels as if it's beyond hope. But is it really? It feels foreign to consider that better days await or that happiness is something you will feel again. Trust the One who fills you, even when you don't feel the filling. In Christ's love, you are "filled with all the fullness of God" (Ephesians 3:19).

> **R&R:** To which one of these feelings (*hurt*, *empty*, or *hopeless*) do you relate the most, at least right now? Why?

❖ You are *hurt*, but healing is on its way. Read Psalm 147:3.

❖ You feel *empty*, but you can trust that you are receiving an abundant refill of the best kind. Read Romans 15:13.

❖ Are you *hopeless*? No! Why? Because you have hope in the Savior who loves you and provides eternal comfort by His grace. Read 2 Thessalonians 2:16–17.

When your soul is downcast, cling to the sure and certain hope that is yours in Christ. Praise Him in every situation. He hears you. He holds you. He helps you. He is your salvation and your God! The psalmist continues, "Hope in God; for I shall again praise Him, my salvation and my God" (Psalm 42:5–6).

When Jesus told Martha, "I am the resurrection and the life" (John 11:25), He provided the ultimate reassurance of hope for the weary, grieving soul. Death does not have the last word. It does not have the victory. It has lost its sting (see 1 Corinthians 15:54–55). Find refuge in the One who restores your soul and continues to minister to it. He provides ultimate reassurance.

AND ONE MORE THING, FOR WHEN YOU'RE SAD

I know that on my worst, no good, very sad, hardest days, I can still cope. How do I know this? Because the life-giving, life-changing Spirit of God is giving me the willingness and ability to stand strong and not buckle under the burden of the storm. He gives me resolve not to run from my circumstances to an unhealthy or destructive means of escape.

By faith, I possess the resurrection power of Jesus (Ephesians 1:19–20), enabling me to face heartache head-on, meeting confrontation with courage and pain with perseverance—even when it's acute. I am not alone (see Colossians 1:27), and I believe I am richer for having faced the most difficult of circumstances, for my faith has been tested and stretched. Through the storms, I grow stronger, even steadfast.

Jesus invites you to give Him your burdens. The reason for your sadness is real. Your storm may be severe. It's serious stuff, and it's tough. But you do not weather the storm or carry the burden alone. He can and will bear the weight of the load if you let Him. Lean into His lead. Learn from Him. Receive His rest.

> **R&R:** Rest in these words of Jesus right now: Matthew 11:28–30.

BE STILL

My singer-songwriter friend Wendysue penned the words to this beautiful song when she was in college. They resonated with her then; they still speak to her today. As you read the lyrics, note the storm imagery and visualize God's presence. May the words provide you with peace, rest, and reassurance.

"Do not be afraid," said He.

"You can always count on Me.

When your eyes can't find the light,

When you're swallowed by the night,

I'm the guiding star you'll see.

"Although sometimes the storms may rave
And try to drown you in their waves,
The wind and sea obey My will.
When I speak, they become still.

"So when you've lost control,
Give Me the wheel.
I'll take you where you need to go.
I've marked the path for you with footprints in the sod.
So be still,
Be still,
And know that I am God.

"If you lean upon My strength,
We can make it any length.
I will catch you when you fall, and I'll be with you through it all.
My child, don't you forget:
I will see that every need you have is met.
There is no earth or sea for you My feet won't trod.
So be still,
Be still,
And know that I am God.

"I am God, and I know what's best.
Come, lean upon My breast
And I will give you rest.

"Please believe
That you can always count on Me.
My child, be still."[107]

DISCUSSION QUESTION 3 According to the song, what strengths, qualities, and actions of the Lord enable you to be still?

> **R&R:** "God is our refuge and strength, a very present help in trouble" (Psalm 46:1). In light of all you've learned in this week's session, in what ways can you say that Jesus fulfills these words of the psalmist for you? What does your Refuge's gift of the *resurrection* mean to you? What *reassurance* do you receive, today and every day? What might your response be?

JOURNAL: What one takeaway today enables me to say, "I can be still because I know that He is God"?

VIEWER GUIDE

SESSION 6: STORMS OF SADNESS

Read John 11:1–44.

"Deeply moved" (John 11:33), from the Greek *enebrimēsato*: _____.

How did Jesus deal with His own sadness? How can we imitate Him as we deal with our own?

1. He went away to be alone with _____. We can _____.

2. He moved toward others with _____. We can _____.

3. He _____. We can _____.

4. He _____. We can _____.

In their storm of sadness, Martha and Mary asked for their brother's healing. They received, instead, His _____, along with the _____ of the final resurrection for all who believe. They could be still, and know that He is Lord of life everlasting!

Jesus is the giver of _____, as dramatically demonstrated when He raised the dead. Throughout the Gospel of John, we're given this *reassurance*. Just a sampling from John says:

• "In Him was _____, and the life was the light of men" (John 1:4).

• "Whoever believes in Him may have eternal _____" (John 3:15).

• "For as the Father raises the dead and gives [us] life, so also the Son gives _____" (John 5:21).

• "[He] came that [we] may have _____ and have it abundantly" (John 10:10).

• "[He is] the resurrection and the _____" (John 11:25).

DISCUSS

> God is our refuge and strength, a very present help in trouble. Therefore we will not fear though the earth gives way, though the mountains be moved into the heart of the sea, though its waters roar and foam, though the mountains tremble at its swelling. . . . "Be still, and know that I am God." (Psalm 46:1–3, 10)

As you consider your storms of sadness, what do your roaring waters and trembling mountains look like? How is your storm brewing or blowing in a specific situation? What trouble has come because of this storm?

Can you see God working to calm you or calm the storm, helping you to trust Him in it? How do you know that He is God and R.E.S.T. (*refuge, ever*-present *strength* in *trouble*) in that truth? How or where do you see His help?

READY TO R.E.S.T.?

READ AND REFLECT: What do the Scriptures and this Bible study say about storms of sadness? What do they say about Jesus, your refuge in this storm? What were your biggest takeaways?

EXAMINE QUESTIONS AND EXPLORE ANSWERS: For greater understanding and for application, seek answers in Scripture and meditate upon the personal questions.

SHARE: Tell about your takeaways and your storm, with a group or alone, as you write or pray about them.

TRUST your Refuge, the One who provides *reassurance* and the promise of *resurrection*.

STORMS OF SELF

SALOME—MATTHEW 20:20–28

DAY 1: LISTENING

"I SAY THIS FOR YOUR GOOD"

Mom was talking, but my eyes were elsewhere. She was giving me valuable instruction—trying to teach me a lesson—but I didn't want to hear it, though it was for my own good. My friend Myra remembers her mother's reminders when she was behaving similarly. Myra told me:

> I have a particular image from my past that reminds me of lessons taught and received. When I had misheard, misapplied, or simply not paid attention to a direction my mom had given me, she had a particular way of reminding me. She would take my chin in her grip, turn my face to hers, make me look at her eyeball to eyeball, and she would say, "Listen to me! I say this for your good."[108]

R&R: Can you remember a similar situation of your own? In what settings are you most likely to mishear or misapply an important message today? Is it due to lack of attention? Do you sometimes hear only what you want to hear?

As you read Salome's storm story, you will see that she sought Jesus' full attention. But had she been listening to Him? Had she misheard His words? As you read, look for lessons taught and received.

SALOME'S STORM OF SELF—BASED ON MATTHEW 20:20–28

Salome and her sons had spoken privately of this matter. Now they approached Jesus. Salome knew she would have Jesus' ear. He was unlike any other rabbi. He listened intently to everyone. He welcomed women to follow, learn, and receive a good word from Him. Indeed, Jesus listened to her whirlwind of words: "Say that these two sons of mine are to sit, one at Your right hand and one at Your left, in Your kingdom" (Matthew 20:21).

The best two seats in the house were not too good for her boys. After all, they had served with loyalty and faithfulness beside the Teacher throughout His three-year ministry; in fact, they were two of Jesus' inner circle of three. Not only had they learned under Him, but they had also aided Him as He ministered; they'd been sent out to preach about His kingdom. Jesus had even given them a special term of endearment, "Sons of Thunder" (Mark 3:17). Hadn't Jesus spoken to the Twelve about His kingdom and how all of them would share in His rule?

She envisioned how amazing it would be to have her sons in positions of authority and be men of influence in the messianic kingdom. Could this coming kingdom mean the end of Roman rule? She could only imagine how different her people's lives would be, freed from tyrannical Roman leaders.

Before Salome's thoughts went further, Jesus spoke. With a look of understanding mixed with concern, Jesus gently warned, "You do not know what you are asking. Are you able to drink the cup that I am to drink?" (Matthew 20:22).

Without hesitation, her sons stepped forward. Almost in unison, they replied, "We are able" (verse 22), eagerly nodding, as if to affirm their words. A sad expression came over Jesus' face as He continued with a sigh, "You will drink My cup" (verse 23).

Salome pondered the meaning of this. Why would that trouble Jesus? Wouldn't He want His disciples to share in His glorious reign?

Jesus continued, "But to sit at My right hand and at My left is not Mine to grant, but it is for those for whom it has been prepared by My Father" (verse 23).

The next thing she knew, the other disciples had found out about her request, and they were more than a little miffed. It had been a bold request (and a little self-serving), so she could understand why the other ten apostles were indignant. Did their response reveal that they secretly hoped for the same positions? They, too, had faithfully followed the Teacher.

Jesus contrasted the abuse of Gentile leaders' power over their people with the humble servant leadership that would occur in His kingdom. "Whoever would be great among you must be your servant, and whoever would be first among you must be your slave, even as the Son of Man came not to be served but to serve, and to give His life as a ransom for many" (verses 26–28).

Salome took note of Jesus' necessary but gentle rebuke for what had been a selfish request. Grateful for His grace, she resolved to continue following Jesus, whatever the cost. Though still a mystery for a little while longer, His coming kingdom would be incomparably better than all that she had earlier envisioned.

> **R&R:** Pause to ponder Salome's story. Read Matthew 20:20–28, then write what stood out to you. What was your first and immediate takeaway?

DISCUSSION QUESTION 1 "God is our refuge and strength, a very present help in trouble" (Psalm 46:1). In what ways did Jesus fulfill these words of the psalmist for Salome? How was He her refuge in her storm?

In her storm of her own making, Salome made a self-seeking request on behalf of her sons. She received, instead, a gentle *rebuke*, along with the crucial *reminder* of God's plan and the humble ways of His kingdom.

DISCUSSION QUESTION 2 "Be still, and know that I am God. I will be exalted among the nations, I will be exalted in the earth!" (Psalm 46:10). Picture Salome's life following her encounter with Christ. How do you think these words would have spoken to her? How was Jesus exalted in her life and, through her, into the world? We have hints from the Gospels, as we'll see shortly in our study.

"I SAY THIS FOR YOUR GOOD" WRAP-UP

Myra's mother and my own taught us to listen, for our own good. I'm still learning to listen to the Lord, and Myra is too, as she envisions her mother's reminders, complete with her chin in her mother's grip. Myra continued:

> That image has come to mind [as] I hear God's reminders to me: "In the world you will have tribulation. But take heart; I have overcome the world" (John 16:33). "Let not your hearts be troubled, neither let them be afraid" (John 14:27b). "Call upon Me in the day of trouble; I will deliver you, and you shall glorify Me" (Psalm 50:15). In the midst of our fears, . . . God has taken our chins in His hand and focused our eyes on the assurance in His Word. Listen to Him.[109]

Thanks be to God for His gentle rebuke and His loving reminders.

> **R&R:** Is there a particular verse that leads you to lean in and listen especially closely? Write it here. Envision the Lord holding your chin in His hand as He speaks His Word of truth to you.

JOURNAL: What one takeaway today enables me to say, "I can be still because I know that He is God"?

DAY 2: A BOLD REQUEST

SONS OF THUNDER, AND THEIR MOTHER

All four Gospels identify James and John as sons of Zebedee. Since they all provide the reference, it's likely that Zebedee was a well-known man in the area. Fishing was a profitable livelihood and an important industry for the culture. The family fishing business was located near the Sea of Galilee and was large enough to support hired workers (Mark 1:19–20). James and John were among the first to be called by Jesus, who invited them away from their family business to become "fishers of men" (Mark 1:17). They promptly dropped their nets and followed Jesus, who nicknamed them "Sons of Thunder" (Mark 3:17). They were known for their boldness, so maybe they were a storm to be reckoned with. Could they have inherited that trait from their mother?

> **R&R:** Nicknames are often given to reflect a trait or personality. Have you had a nickname during different times in your life? Do you recognize certain traits that you have inherited?

Along with Peter, these brothers were chosen by Jesus for special purposes. Sometimes referred to as the "inner circle," they were privileged to travel with Him up the mountain where He was transfigured before them (Matthew 17:1–8). Soon after this account, Jesus took the three men into the Garden of Gethsemane to keep watch and pray (Matthew 26:37). While Jesus would not have played favorites, He knew the plans He had for each of His followers, and these plans were unique to Peter and the sons of Zebedee.

Because Salome was also a follower of Jesus, she was one of several women who would have witnessed many amazing things as Jesus traveled. She would have heard and seen Him proclaiming the kingdom of God and miraculously healing, feeding, and forgiving people as He went. Salome, like a few of the other female followers of Jesus, was a strong enough supporter to be mentioned by name more than once. As we learned while studying the stories of Mary and Martha, Jesus welcomed and valued women as followers, in sharp contrast with other Jewish rabbis of His time.

DISCUSSION QUESTION 1 Read Mark 15:40–41 and Luke 8:1–3. What did these women do as they traveled with Jesus throughout His ministry? What does this say about their hearts for Jesus and His mission?

SELFISH MOTIVE?

What was Salome's motive behind her request? Was it merely selfish ambition on behalf of her sons? Or did she just want to ensure that her sons would be cared for? Maybe she was well-intentioned, merely wanting the best for her family, her dearest loved ones. She knew that all Twelve were promised positions of power, alongside Christ, in His coming kingdom (see Matthew 19:28). Maybe Salome and her sons saw an opportunity to ask for more.

DISCUSSION QUESTION 2 If Salome outlived her husband, Zebedee, how would she be provided for, according to Jewish custom? How could that impact her concern for her sons?

IN HIS KINGDOM

In an earthly kingdom, the seats on either side of the king were the seats of power, second only to the king himself. Clearly, Jesus' followers were still confused about His kingdom and mission, for them to make such a request. Jesus told them as much. He said, "You do not know what you are asking" (Matthew 20:22).

Jesus gently rebuked Salome because she *didn't* know what she was asking. Her request revealed that she and her sons perceived Jesus' coming kingdom "as a visible throne surrounded by a clear hierarchy."[110]

THE CUP

"Are you able to drink the cup that I am to drink?" (verse 22). Jesus' question contained so much more than any of them understood at the moment. James and John eagerly answered, "We are able," attempting to guarantee their places and thinking themselves ready for the task (and the privileges, benefits, and glory that would come with it). Was their mother nodding too, hopeful of an affirmative response from Jesus?

> **R&R:** Have you ever made a bold request for something, eager to receive an affirmative answer, since you were already envisioning the benefits this thing would bring your way? Was your request granted? Was it what you thought it would be?

Jesus *did* say they would drink the same cup, but imagine the sadness in His reply. Hardly a king's royal banquet cup, His would be one of suffering. He knew their future would include persecution and suffering, although it would be incomparable to His own. But suffering would come to them, because of Christ and the message of the cross they would proclaim. These were the privileges and benefits for leaders seated with Christ in His coming kingdom. In this way, they would drink the same cup.

DISCUSSION QUESTION 3 Read about the cup to which Jesus referred. All four Gospels contain similar accounts. What was the context? Where did the cup come from? To what did it refer? See Matthew 26:39, 42; Mark 14:36; Luke 22:42; John 18:11.

To "drink the cup" meant to undergo or experience something. In this case, it meant suffering.[111] Throughout Jesus' ministry, He faced suffering of so many kinds:

He was rejected by His hometown.

He withstood wrongful accusations from the religious leaders.

He endured repeated cruel acts against Him.

He was often misunderstood, even by His closest followers.

He was left alone, unsupported, during His hour of great need just before His arrest.

He was beaten, mocked, and spat upon during an unfair trial.

He suffered humiliation as He hung, naked, on the cross.

He was crucified on the Roman tool of torture, the place of His final suffering and death.

Praise Jesus for the cup He took on our behalf. Praise Him for the suffering He endured. Praise Him for the salvation that is ours, thanks to His humble sacrifice at the cross.

JOURNAL: What one takeaway today enables me to say, "I can be still because I know that He is God"?

DAY 3: A GENTLE REBUKE

LOOKING OUT FOR NUMBER 1

How often do I secretly hope that I'll be the first, the best, or the favorite? Do I privately hope I am number 1 on any given list? Okay, sometimes I'm not even so secretive about it. In our human condition of sin, we turn inward on ourselves. We look out for number 1.

As we study Salome's storm, let's also examine the other disciples' responses to the question she asked Jesus. "When the ten heard it, they were indignant at the two brothers" (Matthew 20:24). Why did the request bother them so much? Maybe because they, too, desired to sit in the places of highest honor. Perhaps each wanted to be in the number 1 seat because each was looking out for himself.[112]

Jesus set things straight. "Whoever would be great among you must be your servant, and whoever would be first among you must be your slave" (verse 26). Yes, Jesus' kingdom would be vastly different than those the disciples had known. While they were still imagining a kingdom like the familiar earthly ones, He was communicating the nature of servant leadership and humility.

CLEARING THE CONFUSION

Jesus used Salome's request as another opportunity to impress upon His closest followers the purpose and nature of His coming kingdom. His words were meant to clear any misconceptions of greatness and what it would mean under the reign of Christ the King. A worldly understanding of Christ's kingdom caused Salome to envision power and authority for them, as His next-in-command.

To make clear just how opposite His kingdom would be, Jesus referenced Gentile nations and tyrannical leaders as examples of those who abuse power by exploiting others and dominating. Stormy circumstances of many nations were direct results of corrupt leaders misusing their power. The last thing Jesus would have in His kingdom would be people in positions of power for personal or public gain.

DISCUSSION QUESTION 1 We could extract a phrase or a sentence from the previous paragraph and plop it into a contemporary news piece, describing one of many nations today. What phrase or sentence stands out to you in this way?

THE COMING KINGDOM

Old Testament messianic prophesy proclaimed that the Messiah would restore Israel to self-rule, as in the glory days under King David's reign. This long-awaited Deliverer would bring peace and supply all their needs. The Jews had waited and watched for this Messiah for generations. Presently, they were oppressed under the Roman government, which occupied Israel. The Jews believed that the Messiah would deliver them from this physical and political bondage. But what about other messianic prophesies, the ones that predicted a Suffering Servant, as well as a Deliverer?

> He was despised and rejected by men, a man of sorrows and acquainted with grief; and as one from whom men hide their faces He was despised, and we esteemed Him not. Surely He has borne our griefs and carried our sorrows; yet we esteemed Him stricken, smitten by God, and afflicted. But He was pierced for our transgressions; He was crushed for our iniquities; upon Him was the chastisement that brought us peace, and with His wounds we are healed. (Isaiah 53:3–5)

DISCUSSION QUESTION 2 Examine the prophetic words of this passage. Focus on the action words that reveal how Jesus would suffer. Underline those words or phrases. Note every "He" and mark every "we," "our," and "us," contrasting His actions and ours, and noting His work for us. Which words foretell how Jesus would bear our sins for us? What word or phrase really hits home with you?

THE SUFFERING SERVANT

In Jesus' day, the Jews looked to one aspect of the coming Messiah but ignored the other. It's no wonder that Salome didn't understand. Perhaps she thought, "If He is the Messiah, it will mean great things for my family!"

Following the Messiah who is, instead, the Suffering Servant would mean experiencing some of the same sufferings. Maybe they simply didn't want to listen to what Jesus foretold about His own suffering, so they closed their ears to that portion of God's plan.

> **R&R:** When might we behave as the Jews had here, listening to partial truth and believing only the part we want to hear? Do we ever focus only on the part we're sure will benefit us personally and not bring us harm?

Just prior to Salome's selfish request, Jesus had spelled out (for a third time and in the greatest detail yet) God's imminent plan:

> See, we are going up to Jerusalem. And the Son of Man will be delivered over to the chief priests and scribes, and they will condemn Him to death and deliver Him over to the Gentiles to be mocked and flogged and crucified, and He will be raised on the third day. (Matthew 20:18–19)

DISCUSSION QUESTION 3 How could Salome and her sons fail to understand God's plan, when they had just heard this? Read Jesus' similar words to His disciples in Luke 18:31–34. Why couldn't they understand?

DISCUSSION QUESTION 4 When are you most likely to be focused on the here and now, on earthly things? What do you learn about your heart in Matthew 6:19–21 and in Colossians 3:1–2? What might help you look past fleeting earthly things to a heavenly mindset as you live out the here and now under His authority?

SELFLESS SERVICE

Jesus did not scorn Salome for her request; He tenderly rebuked her and her sons. He met them in their storm and gently showed them the truth. He enabled them to step away from the squall and toward a calmer place, where they could consider His coming sacrifice. Instead of giving Salome what she thought she wanted for her sons, He gave her what she needed. As they learned that day, being *someone* in the kingdom of God meant selfless service, not self-promotion.

Salome received Jesus' words and responded with continued service. She would soon stand at the cross on Calvary's hill, looking upon the Suffering Servant. Three days later, she would attempt to serve Jesus one last time, only to arrive at an empty tomb and receive the angelic message. Her Savior had risen from the dead! (See Matthew 27:55–56; Mark 15:40–41, 16:1–7; Luke 24:1–10.)

Have you considered that Salome's service was an example to her sons? James and John then stayed the path of service, led the Early Church and proclaimed the kingdom of God, and suffered in their own way for their faithfulness (one to his martyrdom, and one exiled).

R&R: What do you want to be remembered for? How does that frame your priorities today? What will your family be able to emulate?

JOURNAL: What one takeaway today enables me to say, "I can be still because I know that He is God"?

DAY 4: SERVICE: SACRIFICIAL AND SELFLESS

SACRIFICIAL SERVICE

> The Son of Man came not to be served but to serve, and to give His life as a ransom for many. (Matthew 20:28)

Jesus, God's own Son, could have demanded or rightfully expected to be served. But He came to serve—to give His life "as a ransom for many" in His greatest and final act of sacrificial service. In this powerful climactic verse of our Matthew 20 passage, Jesus proclaimed again the purpose of His imminent crucifixion, this time in servant terms.

The "ransom" was the price paid to redeem (or buy back) or free a slave. Christ paid the ransom price of His own life to free all humankind from the slavery of sin. ("Many" is a Hebrew idiom that means "all."[113]) His ransom covered everyone.

DISCUSSION QUESTION 1 Apostles Paul and Peter both use "ransom" language in their epistles. Read 1 Timothy 2:5–6; 1 Peter 1:18–19. What words stand out to you? With what were you ransomed?

Followers of Jesus are called to selfless service. In Peter's charge to Church leaders, he said, "Shepherd the flock of God that is among you, exercising oversight, not under compulsion, but willingly, as God would have you; not for shameful gain, but eagerly; not domineering over those in your charge, but being examples to the flock" (1 Peter 5:2–3). Servant leadership is not, nor has it ever been, about the one who leads. It's about how God chooses to reveal Himself to others through the servant leader, for their good and for His glory.

Groping toward self-gain, grasping for power or position, or striving for self-importance will take us in the opposite direction of what we really desire in life. Why? Because self-fulfillment never actually satisfies. Whether it's power, possessions, or position, worldly prestige will provide only temporary, fleeting satisfaction at best.

DISCUSSION QUESTION 2 Read this again: self-fulfillment never actually satisfies. Why do you think that is? Do you agree? Explain your thoughts.

Instead of grasping with clenched hands, let's open our hands to receive and then give to others in response to all that we've freely received in Christ. What could be better than being used by the Lord? He uses us to help the hurting, love the lost, and show others the way to Christ or to a closer walk with Him. There will be sacrifice involved, and some suffering too. How do we know that? Because we serve a Savior who led and gave Himself this way.

> **R&R:** Envision ways that you can give up or set aside your needs for others as you serve selflessly. How can you live your life for the Lord by offering yourself as a living sacrifice (see Romans 12:1)? Do you know a person who's hurting or lost? Who in your life is in need of someone who will show them their Savior? Who could use a listening ear or a note to know that someone cares? Prayerfully consider where the Lord may be leading you to live sacrificially and serve selflessly today.

> **R&R:** As we follow Jesus and serve in His name, we can expect some suffering because we're believers. How have you suffered for Jesus' sake? How have you seen others suffer? What good has come from it?

DISCUSSION QUESTION 3 Jesus Himself spoke about the suffering His followers would face for the sake of the Gospel. The apostles Peter and Paul wrote about the suffering of believers for the sake of Jesus. Read John 15:18–21; 1 Peter 4:12–14; 2 Corinthians 4:16–17. Notice the specific ways that suffering is mentioned. What may happen to you because you believe in, follow, and worship Jesus? What bright spots do you see in all this talk of suffering?

HUMBLE SERVICE

The Lord calls humble what the world calls weak, but what a marked difference there is between the two! In humility, we admit our need for the Lord, who gives us His strength. It's in humble service that we best reflect the image of Christ and the love of God. We submit to His authority both when we serve and when we lead by example.

DISCUSSION QUESTION 4 We lead well when we are serving in humility. Read John 13:4–5, 12–15. What menial act of service did Jesus perform for His disciples?[114] What was He teaching through this?

Jesus lived what He taught, which takes us right back to His words to Salome and His disciples: "The Son of Man came not to be served but to serve, and to give His life as a ransom for many" (Matthew 20:28).

It's worth noting that as Jesus was teaching humility and leading by serving, the apostles were seeking power and prestige. Also notable is the mention of Jesus' hands, metaphorically, in Salome's request that her sons would sit at the right and left hands of Christ.

HIS HANDS

The actual hands of Christ had broken bread and blessed it, miraculously feeding thousands.

His hands had humbly washed the disciples' feet.

His hands had cupped the face of the sick and leprous and were repeatedly lifted to the Father in prayer.

Jesus' hands had compassionately taken other people's hands in His.

His hands were bound, stretched out, and nailed to a cross. Two men were at Jesus' right and left hands that day. Not James and John, but criminals hung on either side of Him. Finally, victoriously, Jesus appeared again to James and John and all of His disciples, showing them His nail-scarred hands and confirming His resurrection from the dead.

> **R&R:** Open your hands and stare at them, palms down, then palms up. As you envision all that your Savior's hands have done for you, clasp your hands in prayer and ask Him how you can serve others with your hands today.

JOURNAL: What one takeaway today enables me to say, "I can be still because I know that He is God"?

. . . .

. . . .

DAY 5: A LOVING REMINDER

GREATNESS REDEFINED

When my husband was a student at the seminary, I attended my first women's retreat. Hosted and led by professors' wives, the retreat provided a special spiritual growth opportunity for the wives of seminary students. These were the first women God used to fan into flame my passion for retreat ministry, writing, and speaking. Renee, Lisa, Tonya, and Ginny were godly examples, selflessly serving as they led us in God's Word.

By our fourth and final year, I knew these mentor women well, so I made a bold request to be a part of the retreat planning team. I had gotten my feet wet, so to speak, leading various women's events on campus. I felt certain I could lead! They gladly added me to the team, and then found the perfect role for me: gathering bathroom supplies and stocking the cabins. Well, it wasn't exactly what I'd had in mind. I had dreamed of leading a devotion. But it was the best task they could have given me. While humbling at the time, that task brought me joy, and I prayed it blessed others. As I followed my mentors' lead, I learned to lead by humbly serving first.

> **R&R:** List ways in which you have led (teaching, administrating, leading a committee, and so on). Next to it, list your humble acts of service (cleaning, following orders, performing menial tasks, and such). Is one list greater than the other? Why? Think about your lists in the context of redefining greatness.

Jesus redefined greatness in His gentle rebuke and loving reminder concerning the coming kingdom. "Whoever would be great among you must be your servant," He said, "and whoever would be first among you must be your slave" (Matthew 20:26–27). In other words, a person in authority would assume the role of a servant.

The disciples' obedience in their servant leader roles eventually cost them their lives. All would be martyred but John, who was exiled until his death. James was beheaded for his faith (Acts 12:2). The first and the last to die, the Sons of Thunder bookended the deaths of the apostles.

Humankind's notion of greatness and God's definition of greatness stand in direct contrast. The standard for greatness in the kingdom of God has nothing to do with power or gain. Instead, the standard against which all greatness would be measured is the cross. Greatness is fully revealed and personified in the perfect Son of God. "The measure of all greatness is the self-giving greatness of the Son of Man who serves to the utmost, to the giving of His life for the ransoming of the 'many'."[115]

DISCUSSION QUESTION 1 "Jesus speaks in the language of competitive advantage, catching the interest of the disciples. In Christ's kingdom, positions of authority carried a servant's job."[116] Contrast worldly greatness with Jesus' teachings about greatness in the kingdom of God. Examine these passages: Matthew 19:30; Matthew 20:16; Matthew 20:26–28; Matthew 23:11–12; Mark 9:33–35.

Find contrasting words in each reference, and insert them in the columns.

WORLDLY GREATNESS	KINGDOM GREATNESS

DISCUSSION QUESTION 2 Read Philippians 3:14–21. Where should we set our minds? Where should we not? Read it again, applying it in practical ways as you think of an average day. How can you practice this mindset?

Our culture praises personal ambition and self-interest for self-gain and even self-glory. We may even think ourselves to be self-made because we've given our all to be the best version of ourselves we can be.

DISCUSSION QUESTION 3 Again, our Lord provides a loving reminder of His ways in His Word. In Philippians 2:3–4, what does the Lord say about self-interest, others' interests, and humility? What do we learn about perfect humility in Philippians 2:5–8?

While we may look up admiringly at people whose self-motivation drove them to the top, we have to wonder if their legacies will last. May we look, instead, to those who live out the Lord's loving reminder, redefining greatness in these ways:

❖ Giving priority to those whom they are called to raise, teach, or train

❖ Making a difference in the lives of others, for their physical, mental, emotional, or spiritual good

❖ Inspiring people by their kindness or generosity

❖ Encouraging others to try something new or to step out of a comfort zone

❖ Glorifying Jesus with their time, talents, and possessions

❖ Letting others receive the biggest, the best, or the last portion, even when it means going without

R&R: Read aloud the opening phrase of each godly example above. Do you feel inspired to go and do likewise? Which ones resonate most right now? Why?

R&R: "God is our refuge and strength, a very present help in trouble" (Psalm 46:1). In light of all you've learned in this week's session, in what ways can you say that Jesus fulfills these words of the psalmist for you? What does your Refuge's gentle *rebuke* mean to you? What are the loving *reminders* He provides through His Word: His plan and the humble ways of His kingdom? What might your response be?

JOURNAL: What one takeaway today enables me to say, "I can be still because I know that He is God"?

VIEWER GUIDE

SESSION 7: STORMS OF SELF

Maybe you've created a storm of self, allowing self-_____, selfish _____, or self-_____ to seep inside.

Turn to Matthew 20:20–28.

In her storm of self, Salome made a self-seeking request on behalf of her sons. She received, instead, a gentle _____, along with the crucial _____ of God's plan and the humble ways of His kingdom.

Self-fulfillment never truly _____.

By God's grace, we can live _____, serve _____, and show others the way to Christ or to a closer walk with Him.

How can we be like Salome?

- May we be faithful _____ of Jesus, serving sacrificially and ministering to others' needs.

- May we pray to keep our eyes on Calvary's cross, remaining _____ and steadfast in our faith, even if others depart in fear.

- May we take every opportunity to tell the _____ _____ of Jesus' resurrection and of the final resurrection for all who believe!

DISCUSS

> God is our refuge and strength, a very present help in trouble. Therefore we will not fear though the earth gives way, though the mountains be moved into the heart of the sea, though its waters roar and foam, though the mountains tremble at its swelling. . . . "Be still, and know that I am God." (Psalm 46:1–3, 10)

As you consider your storms of self, what do your roaring waters and trembling mountains look like? How is your storm brewing or blowing in a specific situation? What trouble has come because of this storm?

Can you see God working to calm you or calm the storm, helping you to trust Him in it? How do you know that He is God and R.E.S.T. (*refuge, ever*-present *strength* in *trouble*) in that truth? How or where do you see His help?

READY TO R.E.S.T.?

READ AND REVEAL: What do the Scriptures and this Bible study reveal about storms of self? What do they say about Jesus, your refuge in this storm? What were your biggest takeaways?

EXAMINE QUESTIONS AND EXPLORE ANSWERS: For greater understanding and for application, seek answers in Scripture and meditate upon the personal questions.

SHARE: Tell about your takeaways and your storm, with a group or alone, as you write or pray about them.

TRUST your Refuge, the One who provides a gentle *rebuke* with His loving *reminders* of truth.

STORMS OF SORROW

MARY MAGDALENE—LUKE 23:55–24:12;
JOHN 19:25–27; 20:1–2, 11–18

DAY 1: FACING TOMORROW

WHAT SORROW FEELS LIKE

Have you ever wondered how you can face a new day? Does fear stare you down in the dark? Have you questioned if the future can possibly hold anything good?

When sorrow settles in, it can keep you from sleep and lead you to wonder if you'll ever feel better again. If you've ever been overwhelmed by loss, devastated by a disaster, or weighed down by defeat, you know what sorrow feels like. Maybe you can relate, on some level, to the sorrow felt by Mary Magdalene.

MARY'S STORM OF SORROW—BASED ON LUKE 23:55–24:12; JOHN 19:25–27; 20:1–2, 11–18 (SEE ALSO MARK 15:40–41)

She couldn't sleep. A heaviness permeated her soul, much as the darkness still saturated the predawn sky. Mary lay awake again, overwhelmed with memories. Before Jesus had entered Mary's life, it had been chaos. Seven demons had dominion over her body, and every day, they frightened and tormented her from within, producing only misery and pain (Luke 8:2). But then her Deliverer came. He commanded the demons to leave her, and instantly, they were gone. For the first time in years, Mary was in her right mind. From that moment forward, she wanted nothing more than to follow this man, the Teacher, who had saved her from her storm of satanic possession.

Her healing happened early in Jesus' ministry, while He was still in Galilee near her hometown of Magdala. So, as He and His band of disciples traveled, Mary went with them. She and a handful of other women, all profoundly grateful for His compassion and healing, sought to help Jesus and the disciples as they traveled together, providing for them out of their own means.

Mary and the other women heard Jesus' remarkable messages about God's kingdom. He was unlike any teacher of His time, for He welcomed women into His fold and treated them with the same benevolence and respect He showed to men. They witnessed His many healings and other miracles; they saw Him bring peace and compassion to countless people. Like every devoted follower, they loved Him, their Teacher and their Lord.

Multitudes followed Jesus. Just days ago, crowds had filled the entrance to Jerusalem, hailing Him as King and shouting, "Hosanna! Save us!" Mary had stood among them, rejoicing that her Deliverer had come—not only for her but also for the nation.

And then, a few days later, in a matter of mere hours, everything had changed. Jesus was arrested, tried, and sentenced to death.

Mary couldn't erase from her mind the horrific sights and sounds that had followed. The religious leaders had made false accusations to incriminate Jesus. Then came the sickening response from the crowd: "Crucify Him!"

Mary winced as she recalled the mocking words of the Roman guards as they had struck Jesus and spat on Him. Her tears fell again as she remembered how the blood had trickled down Jesus' back while He had been beaten. Then He had been forced to carry the cross bar to Calvary's hill. She had followed, clinging to the other women, weeping and wailing with them as they mourned for Him and grieved their own horrifying loss.

A slow chill crept across Mary's body as she recalled the worst of it all: the crucifixion. Despite how gruesome it was, she and the others could not tear themselves away. They needed to stay near Jesus until the bitter, awful end. Oh, the humiliation of her Lord, as He was stripped and hung before a mixed crowed of mockers and mourners. She had covered her ears, hoping to block the sound as large square spikes had been pounded through His hands and His feet. In her mind, she could still see the sign hung above His head, mocking Him: "Jesus of Nazareth, the King of the Jews" (John 19:19). She could still hear the shouts and the sneers, "Save Yourself!" (Luke 23:37). Most memorable had been Jesus' own words, spoken amid His agony and out of love for all.

He had asked for the Father's forgiveness of those who had placed Him there (Luke 23:34).

He had promised salvation to the sorry sinner nailed next to Him (Luke 23:43).

He had looked on His mother during His own time of suffering and provided for her, so great was His compassion (John 19:26–27).

He had cried out as one forsaken by God the Father (Matthew 27:46; Mark 15:34).

He had groaned with thirst (John 19:28).

He had commended His spirit to the Father (Luke 23:46).

And then He had exclaimed, "It is finished" (John 19:30). The sky had grown dark; the earth had rumbled and then shook.

That was three days ago. With another sob, Mary whispered, "It is finished." It was. He was dead.

Mary's thoughts took her back to what had happened when it was over. She and the others had watched on, still sobbing, as a soldier had thrust a spear into Jesus' side, ensuring His end. Then two men had come forward—religious leaders, but secretly followers of Jesus too. One had received the Roman governor's permission to anoint and bury Jesus' body. Mary and a few others had followed them to see where they would bury the Lord after wrapping His body with linens and spices. It had been nearly sundown, when the Sabbath would begin, so the proper burial had to wait. Mary had gone home, prepared more spices, and resolved to return to the tomb following the Sabbath.

And now the time had come. Mary rose before dawn. She gathered the spices and started for the tomb, meeting the other women along the way. The somber journey came to an abrupt stop at sunrise as they neared the tomb and saw that the sealed stone had been rolled away. Mary's thoughts swirled. Who would dare to disturb the grave? Trembling, she moved to the entrance and peered inside. Where was the Lord? Mary had seen for herself that Jesus' body had been laid there, but now it was gone!

Suddenly, two men appeared in the tomb—angels in white robes, whose brilliance filled the shadowed space. The women fell to the ground in fear, bowing before them, only to hear them say the unbelievable: "Why do you seek the living among the dead? He is not here, but has risen. Remember how He told you, while He was still in Galilee, that the Son of Man must be delivered into the hands of sinful men and be crucified and on the third day rise" (Luke 24:5–7).

Could it be true? Was it too much to hope for?

The women hurried back to town, away from the grave and toward the disciples, with the most incredible message. As soon as Mary shouted the news, Peter and John took off for the tomb to see for themselves.

Later, Mary returned to the tomb. Staring inside, she started to weep. Perhaps the news had been too good to be true. Perhaps His body had been stolen by grave robbers or by His enemies.

Still confused and sobbing, she was interrupted by an angel's words, "Woman, why are you weeping?" (John 20:13). She answered that her Lord's body had been taken. Then she turned to see someone else standing near. Was it the gardener, perhaps?

"Woman, why are you weeping?" the man said, echoing the angel's question. He continued. "Whom are you seeking?" (verse 15). With another sob, Mary said, "Sir, if You have carried Him away, tell me where You have laid Him, and I will take Him away" (verse 15).

He replied with one word that changed her world forever: "Mary" (verse 16).

Gasping, she stared into the face of her resurrected Lord! As the sun rose that Sunday morning, the light of the Son shone, dispelling all darkness and every storm that led to death. He was alive! Running to Jesus, Mary embraced Him, crying, "Rabboni!" (verse 16). *Teacher*. Again, she wept, but this time for joy. Desperate to keep Him from ever leaving again, she clung to Jesus' feet as she cried in relief. She knew He understood her emotions, even as He then gently redirected her with special instructions: "Do not cling to Me, for I have not yet ascended to the Father; but go to My brothers and say to them, 'I am ascending to My Father and your Father, to My God and your God' " (verse 17).

This time, she could proclaim with certainty that Jesus had risen. "I have seen the Lord" (verse 18), she told the disciples. Her Deliverer had defeated death. He had called her by name and declared that His Father is also hers, by faith! He would soon ascend to the Father in heaven, but not before Mary could proclaim to the world what she had seen for herself.

> **R&R:** Pause to ponder the story of Mary Magdalene, also reading Luke 23:55–24:12; John 19:25–27; 20:1–2, 11–18. Write what stood out to you. What was your first and immediate takeaway?

DISCUSSION QUESTION 1 "God is our refuge and strength, a very present help in trouble" (Psalm 46:1). In what ways did Jesus fulfill these words of the psalmist for Mary Magdalene? How was He her refuge in her storm?

In her storm of sorrow, Mary had seen her Savior crucified. Then she had gone to the tomb, expecting to serve Him one last time. She received, instead, news of His *resurrection*, a *reunion* with Jesus Himself, and a *restored* relationship with God the Father, through Christ's sacrifice and victory!

DISCUSSION QUESTION 2 "Be still, and know that I am God. I will be exalted among the nations, I will be exalted in the earth!" (Psalm 46:10). Picture Mary Magdalene's life after her encounter with the resurrected Christ. How do you think these words would have spoken to her? How was Jesus exalted in her life and through her into the world?

FACING TOMORROW AGAIN

Recall the questions at the start of this session. Then read on to receive a good word from my friend Sarah, who shared the following words with me immediately after Easter:

> We are called now more than ever to not just know that He lives but to live today as a result! Are we living, knowing we can face tomorrow? . . . Are we living, confidently knowing, "He's got the whole world in His hands"? Are we living, knowing He has overcome? Today, may His Spirit spur you on toward a life that lives because He lives![117]

R&R: In God's strength and by His grace, you can face tomorrow. What might that look like for you? Remember, *the One who lives* has you in His hands.

JOURNAL: What one takeaway today enables me to say, "I can be still because I know that He is God"?

DAY 2: SHARING IN HIS SORROW—SAFE IN HIS HANDS

LIVING PROOF

Most of what we know about Mary Magdalene is found in the four Gospels' crucifixion and resurrection accounts. Her name is mentioned thirteen times; the only woman mentioned by name more often is Jesus' mother, Mary.

We first meet Mary Magdalene when Jesus stepped into her tormented life early in His ministry (recorded in Luke 8:2). He came to her in her personal storm of demon possession, and He cast the demons out. "In a word, possibly a touch, or maybe as He called her by name, the demons were removed and replaced with a peace never before known."[118]

Mary was living proof of God's power over horrifying storms. Imagine the immediate impact upon those who had known her only as the woman to avoid—the mad woman, possessed by seven demons. Her changed life was witness to God's miraculous work in His fulfillment of prophesy: He would "loose the bonds of wickedness, . . . to let the oppressed go free" (Isaiah 58:6). Jesus delivered Mary from spiritual bondage, giving her new life, and she responded by committing her life to Him with devoted service.

FAITHFUL FOLLOWERS

Mary and several other women accompanied Jesus in His travels (Luke 8:1–3), ministering to His needs with service and financial support. Doing so meant breaking cultural norms and barriers: "In Jewish tradition, females were not normally allowed to study and become disciples of a rabbi."[119] Recall a similar situation, when Mary of Bethany learned at Jesus' feet and He defended her for it (see Session 5). Jesus welcomed women. In fact, "female disciples [made] important contributions to Jesus' ministry and God's unfolding plan of salvation for all people."[120] These women were faithful followers from the early days of Jesus' ministry and all the way to the end of His life. All four Gospels make special mention of them: Matthew 27:55–56; Mark 15:40–41; Luke 23:49; John 19:25.

Like every disciple, Mary and the other women risked possible persecution because they publicly followed Jesus. They took up their crosses daily and followed Him (see Luke 9:23). They risked much and loved much, and at His death, they suffered much. They must have cried in shock at the injustice of the trial. They surely gasped in horror as Jesus was beaten and tortured. They certainly wept in sorrow as He was crucified at Calvary. "While the other disciples (except John) cowered in fear, the women stayed to witness the events."[121] How horrifying to witness the intense suffering of the One who had loved them beyond measure and changed their lives forever.

JESUS' STORM OF SORROW

Marlys Taege Moberg wrote:

> Jewish law prohibited more than forty lashes, but the Romans may have administered more. They used a whip of leather thongs with lead balls knotted into the ends. As the blows cut the skin, blood would begin oozing from the victim's body. . . . So severe were these beatings that victims often died before they could be crucified.[122]

Crucifixion was the most painful torture invented as a death sentence. The word *crucifixion* shares the same Latin origin as *excruciating*, describing intense suffering, torment, torture, and unbearable distress.[123] As the women watched, their sorrow must have been more than they could bear, but what a testimony it was to the depth of their devotion.

I pray we never have to witness a loved one face torture, but perhaps you have watched a loved one suffer through final moments in agony, and you know how excruciatingly painful it is.

At Jesus' final breath, sorrow blanketed Mary Magdalene and the others, even as darkness filled the midday sky. The quaking earth could not compare to the storm their Lord experienced on the cross or the despair and sorrow that shook them to the depths of their souls.

In your own storms of sorrow, listen to Isaiah's prophetic words that Jesus would be "a man of sorrows and acquainted with grief. . . . Surely He has borne our griefs and carried our sorrows; yet we esteemed Him stricken, smitten by God, and afflicted" (Isaiah 53:3–4).

Today's study contains no numbered questions, and you'll soon see why. The seven statements of Christ at the cross provide space to rest and reflect (R&R) today.

> **R&R:** Look to Jesus' last words. Read aloud the personal applications. Then look up the additional verses and write your reflections connected to each one.

"FATHER, FORGIVE THEM, FOR THEY KNOW NOT WHAT THEY DO" (Luke 23:34). Jesus cried out to the Father on your behalf. Jesus intercedes to the Father for you. Trust Him to hear you, answer every cry, and forgive every sin.

Isaiah 53:12

Hebrews 7:25

"TRULY, I SAY TO YOU, TODAY YOU WILL BE WITH ME IN PARADISE" (Luke 23:43). When your sorrow runs deep, know that the one whose loss you grieve is now, by faith, with Jesus. You, too, have the promise of an eternal reunion with your loved one and with your Lord.

John 14:1–3

Philippians 1:23b

"WOMAN, BEHOLD, YOUR SON!" (John 19:26). Just as Jesus arranged with John to care for His mother in her time of sorrow and loss, He knows your everyday needs, from the smallest to the greatest, and He provides for them.

Matthew 6:31-33

Philippians 4:19

"MY GOD, MY GOD, WHY HAVE YOU FORSAKEN ME?" (Mark 15:34). Jesus took the rightful wrath of God in your place. He was forsaken so that you will never be! Even when it feels like God is far off, even if it seems that He has forsaken or forgotten you, He never could, and He never will. He is with you.

Deuteronomy 31: 6,8

Hebrews 13:5

"I THIRST" (John 19:28). Jesus revealed again that He was fully man, even as He was fully God. He understands your bodily, emotional, and spiritual needs. Are you weak, anguished, or thirsty in more ways than one? He knows. He's been there. He understands.

Luke 22:44

John 4:6

"'IT IS FINISHED,' AND HE BOWED HIS HEAD AND GAVE UP HIS SPIRIT" (John 19:30). Jesus declared these final words personally for you, for every person at the cross that day, and for all believers of all time. Your sins and mine led Him to the cross because He knew we could not save ourselves. His love compelled Him to go. "It is finished" was a victory cry: His salvation work on your behalf was finished when He took your sins upon Himself and died in your place. Victory is yours for eternity and for today, no matter what you face or how you feel. Cling to this salvation truth!

1 Corinthians 15:57

1 John 2:2

"'FATHER, INTO YOUR HANDS I COMMIT MY SPIRIT!' AND HAVING SAID THIS HE BREATHED HIS LAST" (Luke 23:46). You are in God's capable hands, even now. Upon your own death and as you mourn the death of others, you can be confident in Christ that the Father receives your soul. You are saved and safe in His hands.

Psalm 73:23

Isaiah 41:13

JOURNAL: What one takeaway today enables me to say, "I can be still because I know that He is God"?

DAY 3: EXPRESSIONS AND EXTENT

EXPRESSING SORROW

Several years ago, I lost my little sister to complications related to her severe special needs. As my parents mourned the terrible loss of their daughter, and as loved ones searched to provide them with words of comfort, my mom and dad expressed their sorrow openly. "She's with Jesus," they said, again and again. Their words of certain hope pointed others to hope as well. This is the hope you and I have. Jesus promised us that our loved ones who die in the faith are at rest with Him, free from the sorrows of this life and home with their Savior. One day, we, too, will be with Jesus. And there is more! We have Christ's promise that He will return on the Last Day, at the final resurrection.

Amid a storm of sorrow, especially sorrow over death, we ache with the pain of our loss. We need to be able to express our sorrow. At the cross, "the crowds . . . returned home beating their breasts" (Luke 23:48) to express their grief.

This study contains no numbered questions. Several expressions follow, leading you to the Word for additional rest and reflection time (**R&R**) today.

> **R&R:** What can you do to express your sorrow and grief? What could help you face it, work through it, and allow God to provide peace and healing in it? As you read each expression, look up the attached verses too. Write a reminder of each, along with your reflections connected to each expression.

❖ *Cry out* to God; He knows what's on your heart already. Express it to Him in words and groans; trust Him to work through them. Read Hebrews 4:16; Romans 8:26–27.

❖ *Communicate* with a pastor, a Christian counselor, and friends who will listen, pray for you, comfort you, or simply weep with you. Read James 5:16; 2 Corinthians 13:11; Romans 12:15.

❖ *Cling* to God's promises, fulfilled in Christ and true for you today. Read 2 Corinthians 1:20; Matthew 28:20; 1 John 5:18; Philippians 4:19; Romans 6:3–5.

❖ *Comfort* others as God comforts you. Trust Him to use another person's stories, experiences, and sorrow to provide healing for both of you. When you offer empathy to another hurting soul, you are both blessed, as you also receive a reminder that you are not alone in your suffering. Read 2 Corinthians 1:3–4.

❖ *Carry on*, in His courage. He has meaningful work for you until He leads you home too. Read 2 Thessalonians 2:16–17; Ephesians 2:10.

If you are sinking beneath a tidal wave of sorrow, know that your Rescuer has come. You have not been left to battle the storm by yourself.

R&R: How can you trust that He is your true refuge in every storm, especially this one? Take a look at the past, present, and future as you ponder each of the following and write reflections:

Peer at His promises kept in the past. How could your study of the Scripture verses above help you to see His work in your life up to this point?

Trust His truth for you today, believing that He can and does work all things together for good (see Romans 8:28), even when you don't see evidence of it in your present state.

Look to the future. The death of a believer is not an end but a new beginning without end. In Christ, you receive eternal life and joy without end. "Weeping may tarry for the night, but joy comes with the morning" (Psalm 30:5).

THE EXTENT OF THEIR SORROW AND OURS

Mary Magdalene and the others could have walked away to grieve in private, but they stayed after other onlookers had gone home. "Family and friends usually remained at the site of execution until the accused was dead."[124] Even after Jesus had breathed His last, the women watched and followed as He was taken to the tomb. Luke 23:55 tells us the women "saw the tomb and how His body was laid." There wasn't time to complete the anointing of Jesus' body before the Sabbath began at sunset. However, the women knew where He had been buried, so they could perform what they thought to be one last labor of love for the Teacher. They made plans to return to the tomb after the Sabbath was over. Then they headed for home to prepare spices for the body while they waited.

Only when we understand their culture and religious laws can we more clearly recognize the extent of their love and devotion for Jesus—and therefore, the extent of their sorrow. The women's commitment to ensure the completion of His burial would mean tending to a body that had begun to decay because of the wait. According to Mosaic Law, those who handled a corpse would be considered unclean for the next seven days (Numbers 19:11–12).

Do we feel the same depth of sorrow as these women when we contemplate our Savior's sacrifice for each of us? Can we grasp the extent of Christ's love, which compelled Him to the cross to die by crucifixion in the place of every sinner? Do we know the limitless length of God's love, which led Him to send His Son? May we have the same depth of sorrow over our sin that Christ did, to lead Him to the cross.

JOURNAL: What one takeaway today enables me to say, "I can be still because I know that He is God"?

DAY 4: SORROW INTO JOY

INSULT ADDED TO INJURY?

R&R: During a difficult time, did something additional happen, adding insult to injury to you or to someone you know? Share.

As Mary and the other women headed toward the tomb before dawn, they had no expectation—no hope—of Jesus' resurrection. They went at the earliest possible opportunity following the Sabbath. "They wasted no time since they believed Jesus' body was decaying."[125]

It's interesting to note that all four Gospels specifically mention Mary Magdalene at the tomb. The differences in the accounts are no surprise, since each Gospel writer focused on different details of the event and on different people. But Mary was singled out in all of them.

When the women noticed that the stone was removed, they ran to the entrance and saw only an empty shelf where Jesus' body had lain. Imagine their swirling thoughts: *Wasn't their sorrow great enough already? Had someone done the unthinkable, stealing the Lord's body? Could they not complete even one last act of love for their beloved Teacher?* It's safe to assume their hearts were racing. Consider how they fairly burst with fear, then cautious joy, as the angels appeared and announced the most wonderful, unbelievable news.

SOUL AMNESIA

The angel helped Mary and the others remember Jesus' prediction of His death and resurrection. "Since these women had accompanied Jesus from Galilee ([Luke] 23:55), they would have heard the recurring predictions Jesus made about His impending suffering and death while they traveled together."[126]

"Soul Amnesia." That's what my friend Karen calls it. She writes:

These words depict what often happens to us as Christian women. Our souls just plain forget. We *know* plenty of truth about God. For starters, we know that God is good. God is faithful. God is loving. God is forgiving. God is preparing a place for us. However, when we are blindsided by the waves of life, our souls often forget. We receive a pink slip, divorce papers, or a diagnosis. Our families struggle with discord and distress. Our workplaces feel more like battlegrounds. We get that phone call or email and life suddenly changes. We worry. We fret . . . and we forget.

Jesus' followers also forgot. In Mark 8:31; 9:31; and 10:32–33, Jesus told His disciples that He would suffer and die in Jerusalem. In each instance, He also shared that He would rise. What were His followers doing after His death? The men were hiding, and the women were fretting about who would roll away the stone for them.

Once Sunday arrived, where should the men have been? At the tomb, looking for a risen Jesus! He told them on three different occasions that He would rise . . . but they forgot. Soul amnesia.

As we encounter the unexpected waves of life, let's remember and focus on what we know about our God . . . especially in those times when Satan, the world, and our flesh tempt us to forget. The cure for soul amnesia? Read God's Word. Thank Him for His character, which never changes. Then, pray with confidence that God will provide![127]

> **R&R:** In our sorrow, sometimes we need a very real reminder of truth, something we may have struggled to hear in a time of confusion or difficulty. Perhaps it is something we have simply forgotten in our grief. We, too, have suffered from soul amnesia. What truth have you shared or received in a storm of sorrow? How did it help?

A SKEPTICAL AUDIENCE

When the women ran and told the disciples what they had seen at the tomb, "These words seemed to [the disciples] an idle tale, and they did not believe them" (Luke 24:11). One translation says, "Their words seemed to them like nonsense" (NIV).

> **R&R:** Put yourself in the women's place: you have the best news ever! You can't wait to share it. You think you will have an attentive audience. But when you share your news, the audience is skeptical. What do you do next? Try again? Give up? Start to doubt the news yourself?

If this happens to you today, trust that God is using your message, regardless of the initial response. Remember that even though the disciples failed to believe, Peter and John were intrigued enough to run and see for themselves.

"MARY"

Maybe Mary had begun to doubt. She had returned to the tomb confused, still sorrowful, and weeping. (Here, the Greek *klaió* means "expressing uncontainable, audible grief or wailing loudly."[128]) But the moments that followed were surely her most memorable, even surpassing those when she was delivered from demons. Again, Jesus came to her in her time of need. He needed only to speak one word, "Mary" (John 20:16).

In a similar way, Jesus speaks to you today. He calls you by name. Realize how personal His message of saving grace is for you: you are known and loved by Him.

DISCUSSION QUESTION 1 Read Isaiah 43:1; Isaiah 49:16; Jeremiah 31:3; Psalm 139:1–2; 1 John 3:1. In your own words, summarize these verses as God speaks these truths to you today.

Perhaps Mary's tears kept her from seeing Jesus clearly. Since she doubted that He was alive, she wouldn't have expected to see Him. It's also possible that Jesus kept Mary from recognizing Him until He spoke her name. "The truth is we are all blind to Jesus until He reveals Himself to us. . . . We know Jesus is our Lord because He revealed it to us through the Holy Spirit."[129]

DISCUSSION QUESTION 2 At other times, Jesus hid Himself from immediate recognition, for His timing and purpose.[130] Read Luke 24:16; John 21:4. What is the context for each?

The Good Shepherd called one of His sheep by name, and she knew His voice at once. She cried, "Rabboni!" (Aramaic for "my lord, my master").[131] Mary's sorrow instantly turned to joy! She went "from rock bottom to heavenly heights" in a matter of moments.[132] In one of His many predictions, Jesus said to His disciples, "So also you have sorrow now, but I will see you again, and your hearts will rejoice, and no one will take your joy from you" (John 16:22).

Mary rushed to embrace Jesus, weeping for joy and clinging to Him! She had thought she would never see her Deliverer again, but He was back. Perhaps she hoped for a return to the way things had been before His death. "The original Greek suggests she meant to continue holding onto Him as though thinking, 'I lost You once; I'll ever lose You again.' "[133] But Jesus let her know she didn't need to worry or keep her hold on Him. He also had a message for her to deliver. She needed to know that "He would not walk and talk with them the same way He had been doing. . . . He would be her ascended Lord. She wasn't going to lose Jesus, but have Him in a new way."[134]

JOURNAL: What one takeaway today enables me to say, "I can be still because I know that He is God"?

DAY 5: RESTORATION

THE ONE THING MISSING

In 2019, Nebraska was hit with what many called "the perfect storm." Timing and temperature mixed with melting snow and heavy rains, resulting in catastrophic flooding in our part of the state.

We watched sorrowfully as the waters receded and the extent of the devastating damage was revealed. Loss took so many forms: cattle and crops, homes, business buildings, roads, and bridges. One heroic man even lost his life while rescuing another victim from the flood.

I prayed, "God, where will You bring good out of this? How will people see You amid all this disaster, loss, and sorrow?"

Our home and small city were spared. We weren't in catastrophic ruins like our rural counterparts, so we said, "This could have been us, but it wasn't. How can we help you?" Our church banded with several others to establish a donation collection site and distribution center to provide resources for affected families. Some people's needs began with the basics of food and household items. Others required buckets, shovels, hazmat suits, and first-aid supplies to assist in the cleanup and begin the process of restoration.

Donations poured in from across the country. Volunteers assisted families as they chose their necessities. But in the midst of the piles of supplies, one volunteer was troubled. "We are missing the one thing people need more than anything else. Hope is the need at the center of all that's missing in people's lives right now," she said. She prayed, "Please, Lord, let someone bring Bibles."

God had a plan in the works already. A week prior, Concordia Gospel Outreach had contacted me to coordinate sending Bibles and children's books to the distribution center.

When my daughter Courtney and I arrived with boxes of Bibles and books, the volunteer burst into tears, telling us she had prayed for that very thing just hours earlier. Courtney embraced and affirmed her while we marveled over God's provision and timing. God knew her heart and the needs of the people long before her prayer. She could cry with the psalmist, "Even before a word is on my tongue, behold, O LORD, You know it altogether" (Psalm 139:4).

We handed out Bibles along with prayers as we provided supplies in the weeks that followed. The community came together, and we could see that God was working! People saw Him when we handed out hope in His name. Through God's Word, hope was restored.

DISCUSSION QUESTION 1 When have you received an answer to prayer, and then learned the Lord was orchestrating that answer for you even before you asked? If He is planning to act already, why pray?

Though we can't see the storms before they form or know what's around the bend before we turn, the Lord can and does. We don't know all the intricate ways He is working, according to His plan and through our prayers, but we trust that He *is* working, and sometimes we get a glimpse, when He allows us to see one of His many ways.

DISCUSSION QUESTION 2 We make plans, but we must trust the Lord's lead. What do Proverbs 16:9 and Proverbs 19:21 tell us about our plans and the Lord's lead? What do they imply about His presence, strength, and help when we are in trouble? How might these wise proverbs also give us comfort?

"IN A MIRROR DIMLY"

1 Corinthians 13:12 reminds us, "For now we see in a mirror dimly, but then face to face. Now I know in part; then I shall know fully, even as I have been fully known." In this life, we see only dimly, as if peering into a mirror. When the apostle Paul wrote this, it made perfect sense that an image was seen only dimly in a mirror, because a mirror—while it provided some reflection—was often only a piece of polished brass or something similar. The image would appear, but it would be blurred at best. We do see God's hand at work, at least in part, and certainly with eyes of faith, by His grace. But we may not fully understand God's will or His ways. We may not know how He will work restoration into a sorrowful situation, but we trust Him at His Word. We know this from verse 12 too: "But then face to face." In the completion of time, when Christ returns, we will finally see Him face-to-face, fully and clearly. We will understand fully what we now know only in part, though even now we are fully known by Him. Although we see only dimly, we are clearly seen by Him.

> **R&R:** When have you seen your Savior work restoration into a sorrowful situation? Trust His continued guidance, by His grace, even when you only see dimly; one day you will see Him face-to-face!

SORROW COMES IN MANY FORMS

Sorrow and grief come in so many forms of loss, such as the kinds that came as a result of the Nebraska floods. Restoration of farmland, homes, and livelihoods are months or years in the making. Sometimes when you suffer loss, it may feel as if you have also lost a part of your identity. Maybe you have lost a relationship by estrangement, divorce, or death. Perhaps your children are grown and have moved away. Maybe you've lost a job or your health.

You've been dealt a crushing blow. When someone or something is taken away that was a large part of who you were and how you spent your time, it is hard to know what to do. You feel as though you don't even know who you are anymore.

Jesus looked with compassion upon Mary Magdalene every time she had need, in every way she suffered. He sees you in the same way. He meets you where you are, battered and beaten by the storm. As your Refuge, He is also your restorer. He calls you by name, reminding you that your identity rests in Him. In Christ, you are a new creation. You may not see the restoration of some precious things you have lost, but He will restore your heart and your hope. Who you are has everything to do with whose you are. When sorrow comes crashing down upon you, remember your true identity in the One who holds you up. The One who restored your relationship to God by His death and resurrection has made you His child. That's who you are, and that will never be lost or taken away.

> **R&R:** Maybe your storms of sorrow have taken many forms too. Rest in the Lord's presence right now. Pray to the One who is your Refuge and your restorer; He is the One who calls you by name. Trust Him to restore your heart and your hope when they've been battered by the storms of sorrow.

HE HAS RISEN!

"He is not here, but has risen" (Luke 24:6). The angel made the first announcement of the greatest news ever proclaimed. Jesus conquered death. Jesus had risen! Jesus IS risen! His resurrection makes our resurrection possible. He ascended to the Father and is, even now, preparing a place for us in His Father's house (John 14:1–3). He is coming back for us. Our graves will be opened, and we will rise to be with the Lord and all believers of all time!

Yes, storms of sorrow rage, sometimes without warning. Sometimes, they will overtake us for a time. When it feels as if we have fallen into the heart of the sea (Psalm 46:2), we trust that He holds our head above the waves. We will not drown in our sorrow. He will turn it to joy. Because Jesus is risen, we can cling with confident hope to His promise of a coming day:

> The Lord Himself will descend from heaven with a cry of command, with the voice of an archangel, and with the sound of the trumpet of God. And the dead in Christ will rise first. Then we who are alive, who are left, will be caught up together with them in the clouds to meet the Lord in the air, and so we will always be with the Lord. (1 Thessalonians 4:16–17)

And God "will wipe away every tear from [our] eyes, and death shall be no more, neither shall there be mourning, nor crying, nor pain anymore, for the former things have passed away" (Revelation 21:4).

R&R: Read John 14:1–3. What do you find most comforting in Jesus' words? Perhaps it is His preparations for you, or the promise of His return. Quietly ponder the eternal joy Jesus has in store for you and every believer.

R&R: "God is our refuge and strength, a very present help in trouble" (Psalm 46:1). In light of all you've learned in this week's session, in what ways can you say that Jesus fulfills these words of the psalmist for you? What does your Refuge's gift of His *resurrection* mean to you? What *restoration* do you receive in Him? What *reunion* awaits you in the final resurrection? What might your response be today?

JOURNAL: What one takeaway today enables me to say, "I can be still because I know that He is God"?

VIEWER GUIDE

SESSION 8: STORMS OF SORROW

Jesus said, "In the world you will have tribulation. But take heart; I have _____ _____ _____" (John 16:33).

What tribulations of the world do you face today? How can you remember to take heart? _____

_____

This world is not our _____. We can't hook our hope to the temporary treasures of this world. What we can do is _____ in a God who has overcome the world.

"You will be sorrowful, but your sorrow will turn into _____" (John 16:20).

Turn to Luke 24:1–12; John 20:1–2, 11–18.

"Rabboni" (John 20:16), from the Greek *rhabbouni*: _____.

In her storm of sorrow, Mary Magdalene saw her Savior crucified. She came to the tomb expecting to serve Him one last time. She received, instead, news of His _____, a _____ with Jesus Himself, and a _____ relationship with God the Father, by Christ's sacrifice and victory!

When sorrow comes crashing down on you, trust Jesus to hold your head above the waves. You will not drown in your sorrow; Jesus is _____. He has overcome the world. He will _____.

John 14:3: _____

DISCUSS

> God is our refuge and strength, a very present help in trouble. Therefore we will not fear though the earth gives way, though the mountains be moved into the heart of the sea, though its waters roar and foam, though the mountains tremble at its swelling. . . . "Be still, and know that I am God." (Psalm 46:1–3, 10)

As you consider your storms of sorrow, what do your roaring waters and trembling mountains look like? How is your storm brewing or blowing in a specific situation? What trouble has come because of this storm?

Can you see God working to calm you or calm the storm, helping you to trust Him in it? How do you know that He is God and R.E.S.T. (*refuge, ever*-present *strength* in *trouble*) in that truth? How or where do you see His help?

READY TO R.E.S.T.?

READ AND REFLECT: What do the Scriptures and this Bible study say about storms of sorrow? What do they say about Jesus, your refuge in this storm? What were your biggest takeaways?

EXAMINE QUESTIONS AND EXPLORE ANSWERS: For greater understanding and for application, seek answers in Scripture and meditate upon the personal questions.

SHARE: Tell about your takeaways and your storm, with a group or alone, as you write or pray about them.

TRUST your Refuge, the One who provides *restoration* by His *resurrection*.

JESUS IS YOUR REFUGE IN THE STORM

REVIEW

BE STILL, AND KNOW THAT HE IS GOD!

In review, can you name specific ways Jesus is our refuge in every type of storm?

SESSION 1

Stormy situations surround us; Jesus, our Refuge, provides _____ in the storms or _____ from them.

SESSION 2

In every storm of sin, Jesus offers _____ and _____, followed by the _____ work He provides daily.

SESSION 3

Jesus provides us with _____. He calls us *daughter*! The ultimate Healer, He provides _____ for body and soul in storms of sickness.

SESSION 4

Jesus comes to the _____ when we're trapped in storms of shame. His living water provides _____ for eternity.

SESSION 5

In storms of scurry, Jesus provides _____, along with the gentle _____ to sit at His feet.

SESSION 6

When storms of sadness hit, Jesus gives ultimate _____ in His promise of the final _____.

SESSION 7

Jesus supplies a gentle _____ when storms of self overtake us. In His Word, He provides loving _____ of His plan and the humble ways of His kingdom.

SESSION 8

In storms of sorrow, we're certain of Jesus' gift of His _____, and our _____ with the Father, as a result. A _____ awaits us in the final resurrection!

ANSWERS

Session 1: *relief, release*

Session 2: *redemption, renewal, renovation*

Session 3: *relationship, remedy*

Session 4: *rescue, refreshment*

Session 5: *rest, redirection*

Session 6: *reassurance, resurrection*

Session 7: *rebuke, reminders*

Session 8: *resurrection, restoration, reunion*

Epilogue

What does every woman across Scripture and every woman today have in common?

We all need Jesus.

We need Him with us in our storms. We need our Refuge, Healer, Helper, and Strength. More than that, we need our Savior, who provides peace with God and saves us from the storm of sin by His forgiveness. And we have Him! He meets us right where we are, whether we are stuck in our storm or have passed through it but have been battered by it. Sometimes He chooses to calm the storm; other times He calms us and holds us close while the storm continues to blow.

Do you know what else we all have in common? We have His complete and undivided attention. He knows everything about us. He listens intently, desires our best, and graciously provides.

Because "Jesus Christ is the same yesterday and today and forever" (Hebrews 13:8), we can confidently say that He is our refuge today just as He was for His followers in the first century. He rescues us from the assaults of others and frees us from our sin. He offers living water and cleanses us from shame. His healing touch is upon us, and His concern is always for us. He weeps with us, gently redirects us, and comforts us in our sorrow.

The Lord reveals Himself, again and again, to be our only true and certain refuge in every storm of life. Do you recognize your need for God at all times, especially in your storms? They will blow you away without Him. When you study the Word of God, He allows you to see your need and how He alone fills that need. He will stay with you through the storm and strengthen you by His Spirit to see the storm through. Be still before Him. Trust Him. Know that He has you in His grip. After all, He is God!

In His mighty power, the Holy Spirit quiets us with His presence and calms us with His comfort, drawing us toward Himself so that we may "be still, and know" (Psalm 46:10). It is during those times of stillness when we stop to pray, when we sit quietly in God's Word, hearing His gentle voice speak to us, that we are reminded again that He is God. He alone has control of all things. He is all-powerful and almighty, defeating sin, death, and the devil at the cross and the empty tomb. By His power at work in us, Christ will be exalted in our lives today and as we await His return!

Therefore God has highly exalted [Jesus] and bestowed on Him the name that is above every name, so that at the name of Jesus every knee should bow, in heaven and on earth and under the earth, and every tongue confess that Jesus Christ is Lord, to the glory of God the Father. (Philippians 2:9–11)

We exalt His name when we proclaim it to other nations; when we speak it to our families, in our churches, and across our communities; and when we live life in Jesus' name, by His grace.

Be still, and know.

DAILY STUDY ANSWERS

SESSION 1

DAY 1

DISCUSSION QUESTION 1 The disciples' physical storm created a storm of fear; they thought they were going to perish. They even doubted His care. Jesus, Lord of all creation, would not fear a storm at sea—or any other, for that matter. Perhaps He planned to provide this lesson in trust for His followers. At any rate, we know that He used the opportunity to perform a miracle of which they were witnesses. He continued to reveal that He was the Son of God.

DISCUSSION QUESTION 2 His words might have resonated with the disciples, who were anything but still or peaceful in that moment. Lacking faith, they were still afraid, but they questioned who Jesus must be, that even the sea obeyed Him. God was working on their hearts. Jesus is working on our hearts; He reveals Himself to us in the Word; He relieves our fears and gives us His peace.

DAY 2

DISCUSSION QUESTION 1 Jesus prophesied His own death at their hands; three days later, He would rise. Without faith, they could not make sense of His words; their thoughts were limited only to the temple in Jerusalem. Jesus, by His death and resurrection, is the fulfillment of all messianic prophesy. He is the fulfillment of Psalm 46; therefore, He is our Refuge, our Redeemer. God is present in Christ, the new temple!

DISCUSSION QUESTION 2 The Egyptian army, in chase of Israel, ran into the parted Red Sea "when the morning appeared" (Exodus 14:27). God worked through Moses to return the parted waves, destroying the army in the sea and saving the Israelites. Similarly, God is in the midst of His city and His people, to help "when morning dawns" (Psalm 46:5), should enemies rage and attack. May the knowledge of God's presence and His power over the enemy give you great comfort. Look to Him, trusting His help; He is your strength!

DISCUSSION QUESTION 3 The refrain of verses 7 and 11 adds to verse 1 in defining God's refuge and presence. In other words, He is our fortress, and He is with us. The psalmist assures us repeatedly of God's protection and presence. Therefore, we don't need to fear!

DAY 3

DISCUSSION QUESTION 1 At the moment of Christ's completed work on our behalf at the cross, the temple curtain was torn in two from top to bottom. It was a miraculous act of God, revealing that Jesus' final and complete sacrifice opened the way for us to follow Him, our forerunner. We have direct access into the presence of God the Father.

DISCUSSION QUESTION 2 "So that we may no longer be children [immature in the faith], tossed to and fro by the waves and carried about by every wind of doctrine, by human cunning, by craftiness in deceitful schemes" (Ephesians 4:14). Your examples may be unique to you.

DISCUSSION QUESTION 3 We share in Christ's victory; by faith, we, too, have overcome the world. "Who is it that overcomes the world except the one who believes that Jesus is the Son of God?" (1 John 5:5).

DAY 4

DISCUSSION QUESTION 1 The Lord is with you wherever you go; He is your strength (Joshua 1:9). He is before you at your right hand (Psalm 16:8). He provides salvation on your behalf; He is with you in the battle (2 Chronicles 20:17). You can be strong and courageous; you don't have to fear, because He is with you. You will not be shaken, because He is at your right hand, leading and guiding you. He calls you to stand firm and hold your position against attacks (on your faith, your family, your future, or others). The Lord fights your battle with you and for you; you do not need to fear or be dismayed.

DISCUSSION QUESTION 2 We are rooted in love (Ephesians 3:17–19). "God is love" (1 John 4:16). We receive this measure of His love and are filled with the fullness of God's love.

DISCUSSION QUESTION 3 "Fear not, for I have redeemed you" (Isaiah 43:1). Words that define you: *redeemed*; *called by name*; *Mine*. Words of imagery: *passing or walking through waters, rivers, fire, and flame.* Your storms, likened to these, will be unique to you, but may include times of faith-testing, persecution, or various trials. In them, God is with you; therefore, they won't overwhelm you, and you will not be burned or consumed by them.

DAY 5

DISCUSSION QUESTION 1 Having received salvation in Christ, you have eternity with Him lying right ahead of you! Christ Jesus is the prize! You can continue relentlessly toward the day of Christ's return, pressing on in His strength, even amid a storm. You can even be optimistic about what lies ahead, knowing it involves God's calling for you and His continued work in you.

DISCUSSION QUESTION 2 Wording will vary but may include the following: God opened the door for Katie to serve at camp all summer, though in an unexpected way. She may have felt better suited or prepared as a counselor, but she trusted God's plan and His faithfulness. From her humbled posture, she recognized all the more her full reliance on Him. He is glorified through every act of ministry and service when they are completed for His glory. Katie was still able to minister to families, and she could see her own growth too.

DISCUSSION QUESTION 3 Isaiah 41:10/Psalm 46 comparison:

"Fear not," "be not dismayed"/"we will not fear" (verse 2).

"I am with you"/"The LORD of hosts is with us" (verse 7).

"I am your God"/"I am God" (verse 10).

"I will strengthen you"/"God is our . . . strength" (verse 1).

"I will help you"/"A very present help" (verse 1); "God will help" (verse 5).

"I will uphold you with My righteous right hand"/"God is our refuge" (verse 1); "our fortress" (verse 7).

SESSION 2

DAY 1

DISCUSSION QUESTION 1 Jesus was her protector from the accusers who sought to stone her. He was her strength in her weakness with sin. He was present with her, helping in her time of trouble. Jesus, her Refuge, provided redemption from sin and renewal for a new life with Him.

DISCUSSION QUESTION 2 Answers will vary but may include the following: freed from her raging storm of sin and condemnation, she could begin a new life filled with peace, filled by her Redeemer. Her changed life (from her demeanor to her choices and more) would reflect the redemption and renewal she had received from Christ.

DAY 2

DISCUSSION QUESTION 1 Your weather-storm story is unique to you. Other answers will vary, but may include the following: We recognize we are not strong enough to withstand or overcome the storm on our own. We seek His forgiveness for it and His help to step away from it. When we hear the roar of thunder (a storm warning), we heed the warning and run away from it. We seek to be mindful and not naive of the scope or dangers of storms, so that we may be guarded against succumbing to them. We pray for God's wisdom to recognize a storm for what it is and admit if and when we are stuck in it. We seek His strength to let go of the sin causing it.

DISCUSSION QUESTION 2 The religious leaders were caught up in sins against Jesus. They were jealous because Jesus was gaining followers and performing miracles and signs. They had malicious intent toward Him because they felt He posed a threat to their power—to their self-righteous, legalistic brand of religious rule. They misused the Law for ulterior motives and treated some people as pawns, such as this woman.

DISCUSSION QUESTION 3 We can imagine that the woman perceived her people's religion to be one of legalistic rules from a God of wrath and condemnation because of what she learned from and received at the hands of the religious elite. If people are led only by Law, they are left condemned (and dead in their sin), because no one can follow the Law perfectly. Caught in a storm of sin, they may be condemned by others and walk away from the faith, believing there is no hope for them. Conversely, they may be fooled into believing they can somehow earn forgiveness and salvation by their observances of the Law (as the legalistic leaders did), thinking that their works could make up for their sins and earn them favor with God.

DISCUSSION QUESTION 4 Maybe the woman's partner had slipped away, or perhaps he was released; either way, he evaded the grip of the accusers and left her to face condemnation alone. We don't know if this was a setup; it certainly plays out like a double standard, since one was accused but not the other. Some scholars believe the woman's partner was part of a plot to trap her. We don't know any of these things for certain; we do know, however, that it was entrapment: the religious leaders caught her with the intention of using her as a pawn before Jesus, in order to entrap Him.

DISCUSSION QUESTION 5 The religious leaders were adhering to the Law only halfway. Mosaic Law stated that both the man and the woman were guilty and deserving the same death sentence.

DISCUSSION QUESTION 6 "For all have sinned and fall short of the glory of God, and are justified by His grace as a gift, through the redemption that is in Christ Jesus" (Romans 3:23–24). Verse 23 states the Law; verse 24 delivers the Gospel. Answers will vary but may include the following: *justified*; *grace*; *gift*; *redemption*; *Christ Jesus*!

DAY 3

DISCUSSION QUESTION 1 Answers will vary but may include the following: "the redeemed woman"; "the woman who received God's grace"; "the woman no longer condemned"; "the woman who was forgiven and free." You are defined not by your sin but by your Savior. The Lord could give you the same or similar words as those you chose to redefine this woman.

DISCUSSION QUESTION 2 We should not sit in judgment of someone for her sins. However, when we recognize a fellow believer's struggle with sin, we can gently call it out, but only after recognizing and repenting of our own (see Matthew 7:5). Our response to another's sin should be motivated by a desire for her repentance and restoration, out of love for that person, and with her best interest in mind.

DISCUSSION QUESTION 3 Jesus provides every opportunity for people to acknowledge their sin, turn from it, and receive His grace by faith, no matter who they are or what they've done.

DISCUSSION QUESTION 4 Wording will vary; one possibility may be as follows: God is patient with us; He desires that all people would repent of their sins, believe, and be saved. Sadly, not everyone will be saved, as some will reject Christ's saving work for them.

DISCUSSION QUESTION 5 While Jesus doesn't excuse or condone sin, He knows our sorry hearts, just as He knows our every act of sin. As we confess our sins, He is faithful to forgive and redeem us!

DAY 4

DISCUSSION QUESTION 1 Your luggage answers will be unique to you. Similarly, our baggage is unique to each of us, but we have all carried it: the guilt from sin. All who believe in Christ are no longer condemned by the guilt of our sins but are free! Formerly dead in our sins, because of God's love for us, we are alive in Christ. Thanks to God's mercy, we don't get what we deserve: condemnation and death. Thanks to His grace, we get what we don't deserve: forgiveness and favor.

DISCUSSION QUESTION 2 God's limitless love is active. Romans 5:8 says that He "shows" His love for us in the greatest of ways: He sent His Son to the cross to cover our debt of sin "while we were still sinners." He knew we could not step out of the storm of sin on our own. He came to condemned sinners, giving us His grace by faith.

DISCUSSION QUESTION 3 God forgives your transgressions and covers your sin (Psalm 32:1). He redeems your life (Psalm 34:22). He removes your transgressions from you as far as the east is from the west (Psalm 103:12). Resonating words will vary. God provides refuge so you won't be condemned.

DISCUSSION QUESTION 4 *Light; old self; new self; spiritual; truth; lies.*

DISCUSSION QUESTION 5 Circle the following: "began a good work" and "bring it to completion" (Philippians 1:16); "works" (Philippians 2:13); "do far more abundantly" and "at work" (Ephesians 3:20–21). By the Spirit's power, we respond to God's work in our lives. By His work, we will and work (that is, desire and do; see Philippians 2:13) according to His pleasure. By His power at work within us, He does incomparably more than what we ask or even imagine. We're working, but it is by God's strength; it is He who works in and through us.

DAY 5

DISCUSSION QUESTION 1 All three verses speak directly or indirectly of transformation, by the Word of God. In His Word, you learn and discern His perfect will through His transforming, renewing work. The Word made flesh, Christ, is the truth that sets you free. Through the Word, the Holy Spirit works transformation in you, molding you into the image of Christ.

DISCUSSION QUESTION 2 Paul does the evil that he does not want to do. He does not do the good that he wants to do. Other answers will vary; as sinners, we can all relate to this struggle with sin.

DISCUSSION QUESTION 3 Paul laments, "Wretched man that I am! Who will deliver me from this body of death?" (Romans 7:24). He rejoices, "Thanks be to God through Jesus Christ our Lord!" (verse 25).

SESSION 3

DAY 1

DISCUSSION QUESTION 1 Jesus was her strength in her weakened, sickly state. He was present with her, helping in her time of trouble. Jesus, her Refuge, provided a remedy to all that ailed her, physically and spiritually. He also provided relationship in the family of God.

DISCUSSION QUESTION 2 Wording will vary. Finally, her twelve-year storm subsided completely with His healing. She could be still and resume life, knowing that He is God, her Savior! By evidence of her healing, He was exalted in her life immediately and to the world around her, as she likely continued to share what He had done.

DAY 2

DISCUSSION QUESTION 1 Touch is significant, because an unclean person was forbidden to touch or be touched. Jesus' healing happened through touch. Though she touched Him, it was solely by His power—His miraculous touch—that she was healed. Not only was He not defiled by her touch, but she was also made clean!

DISCUSSION QUESTION 2 Jesus had healed crowds of people with just a touch. She had likely heard of these healings and believed He could do for her what He had done for them.

DISCUSSION QUESTION 3 (1) Strength suddenly surged through her body; (2) she received immediate healing (the blood flow stopped instantly); and (3) Jesus felt the power go out from Him.

DISCUSSION QUESTION 4 Your answers will be unique, but may be like mine: I imagine my heart pounding in my ears as fear seizes me, thinking I'll be found out by the crowd and cast out because I'm unclean. I think I would be terrified, as she was, trembling and even stumbling in my unsteadiness as I step forward to speak.

DAY 3

DISCUSSION QUESTION 1 The woman could resume relationships and return to public worship. She could return to the marketplace and resume a normal life in general.

DISCUSSION QUESTION 2 Jesus' words clarified the source of her healing. It wasn't by some superstitious notion or any other possible misinterpretation. Jesus' miraculous power alone healed her.

DISCUSSION QUESTION 3 Every promise of God finds its yes in Christ (2 Corinthians 1:20).

DISCUSSION QUESTION 4 You are God's redeemed, adopted daughter in Christ. By the Holy Spirit, you call Him, "Abba! Father!" (Romans 8:15). As His child, you are an heir of the kingdom, chosen and loved, according to His purpose and for His glory.

DISCUSSION QUESTION 5 Answers will vary but may include the following: God's love for me is so great that He calls me His child (1 John 3:1–2). There is nothing that can separate me from His love (Romans 8:38–39). I share in the inheritance of the Father; through His Son, I receive the forgiveness of sins (Colossians 1:12–14). He provides all my needs through His riches in Christ (Philippians 4:19). As a Father, He disciplines me, His child, out of love and for my good (Hebrews 12:5–6).

DAY 4

DISCUSSION QUESTION 1 Peace is possible because it is God's gift to us, a fruit of the Holy Spirit (see Galatians 5:22). Stories will be unique to you.

DISCUSSION QUESTION 2 Jesus looked on people with compassion when He saw "they were harassed and helpless, like sheep without a shepherd" (Matthew 9:36). He knew they needed care and guidance. He taught, proclaimed the Gospel, and healed diseases and afflictions (Matthew 9:35–38). One look at a crowd of thousands, and Jesus had compassion on them, miraculously healing the sick, feeding them, and taking care of their physical needs (Matthew 14:14–21). When Jesus saw the widow of Nain weeping over the death of her son, His compassion led Him to raise her son and give him back to his mother (Luke 7:11–15). Jesus knows your needs and extends His compassion to you out of His love for you too.

DISCUSSION QUESTION 3 Answers will vary, but may include the following: *priceless, invaluable, precious, treasured, redeemed, chosen, remembered, child of God, daughter, heir, loved.*

DISCUSSION QUESTION 4 Answers will be unique to you, but could include the following: we are dependent on God for salvation, forgiveness, faith, physical needs or healing, wisdom, guidance, purpose, spiritual needs or healing, and mental and emotional needs or healing.

DAY 5

DISCUSSION QUESTION 1 Answers will be unique to you. Perhaps you've allowed a lack of healing in the past to weaken your level of trust that God can and may choose to heal you, according to His will. Maybe you limit the scope of your request to physical healing only, not recognizing a greater spiritual need.

DISCUSSION QUESTION 2 God was your strength in your weakness and more. Be specific in your prayer, offering God thanks and praise for His help in your day of distress (see Psalm 59:16).

SESSION 4

DAY 1

DISCUSSION QUESTION 1 Jesus was her strength in her weakness of sin and shame. He was present with her, helping in her time of trouble. He provided her with greatest need: living water, eternal refreshment. Jesus, her Refuge, provided rescue from her storm of shame by His redemption of her sins.

DISCUSSION QUESTION 2 Wording will vary. Jesus rescued her from her storm of shame; she could be still, redeemed and refreshed with living water, knowing that He is Lord of all, both Samaritans and Jews. He was exalted through her witness, almost immediately, as she ran to the townspeople to proclaim what He had done.

DAY 2

DISCUSSION QUESTION 1 You might expect a Jewish rabbi to avoid proximity to you, not to mention contact or conversation. Upon your approach, he would likely leave, to ensure he had not crossed any cultural barriers. Reasons a Jew might avoid going through Samaria included, in part, the following: (1) They despised the Samaritans. (2) They considered the Samaritans an unclean people, and contact could lead to contamination. (3) Entering their territory could cause a hostile encounter.

DISCUSSION QUESTION 2 By His request for a drink, Jesus showed that He was willing to share a cup with a person considered unclean by His people. According to the Law, that would defile Him.

DISCUSSION QUESTION 3 A simple definition of *gift* is "a thing given willingly to someone without payment; a present." The Greek word *dorea* indicates the gift of God's grace through Christ. God willingly offers His grace as a gift, without payment and freely given through Christ's atonement for our sins and shame.

DISCUSSION QUESTION 4 Compassion and empathy make all the difference. Others sought to shame her. Jesus sought to rescue her, bring her to repentance, and provide refreshment of the greatest kind. Once she saw her sin, she could come to repentance, and healing could begin. Shame no longer had a hold on her, because her sin was forgiven. When the Lord reveals His Word to us, our sin is exposed by our failure to keep it. By His grace, we repent, and healing begins. Shame no longer has a hold on us, because our sin is forgiven. He works in our lives, just as He did in hers.

DISCUSSION QUESTION 5 She was likely ostracized and shunned by her community, since she came to the well alone at an unlikely time of day to perform a task that was customarily done as part of socialization. Shame caused isolation. She probably possessed little self-respect, having a history with several husbands and a man she was currently living with. Shame may affect you negatively a number of ways, often including isolation and a lack of self-respect. If shame needs judgment, silence, and secrecy to survive, then empathy and compassion gently open what was held in silence or secret; they replace judgment with grace.

DISCUSSION QUESTION 6 God knows me fully: my thoughts, my heart, my needs (Psalm 94:11; Acts 1:24). He knows my words before they are on my tongue (Psalm 139:1–4). He even knows the number of hairs on my head (Luke 12:6–7)! Answers will be unique but may include the following: I cannot hide anything from the Lord, who knows all. I can come to Him in honesty, with vulnerability, and trust His forgiveness and grace. He is compassionate and understanding, and He desires that my thirst be quenched by Him daily.

DAY 3

DISCUSSION QUESTION 1 While we cannot know a person's heart as Christ does, we can offer a person the same undeserved grace that Christ gives. We should never justify or excuse sin, neither our own nor another's, but we're also not called to dwell on it or judge it. Offering forgiveness from sin does not mean we are ignoring it;

actually, it means we're addressing it. Even if we don't receive an explanation, we can offer empathy, a listening ear, and grace.

DISCUSSION QUESTION 2 Jesus loved her! He knew everything about the woman: her lifestyle, her past, and her shame—the reasons she was at the well in the middle of the day. He wanted her to know that He had come to her amid her sin and shame with the offer of salvation. He revealed to her that He was the long-awaited Messiah from God. He exposed her sin so that spiritual healing could take place through the living water that He offered. By His grace, she received new life; her daily life would take a new turn too, as she immediately witnessed to her community.

DISCUSSION QUESTION 3 Jesus loves you! He knows everything about you, from your inmost thoughts to your hidden sins, shame, and secrets. His love sent Christ to the cross so all of your sin could be exposed to His healing forgiveness. The Law in His Word exposes your sin and reveals your need for a Savior, the living water only He can give. By His grace, you have new life; your daily life takes a new turn too as He continues His good work in and through you.

DISCUSSION QUESTION 4 God seeks those who worship in Spirit—in faith, by the Holy Spirit's power—and truth: the truth of God's Word (see John 4:24).

DAY 4

DISCUSSION QUESTION 1 Maybe you believed you didn't deserve something good because of a secret sin committed in your past, because of an unresolved relationship issue, or because of your impure thoughts. Answers will be unique to you.

DISCUSSION QUESTION 2 We will not be "cast headlong" (Psalm 37:24) because the Lord holds our hand. Your story and His work in you will be unique to you.

DISCUSSION QUESTION 3 He places us on the rock that is Christ, the foundation and cornerstone of our faith.

DAY 5

DISCUSSION QUESTION 1 Water is vital to life and function. Living water is an apt picture, then, for it is an absolute necessity for life! The psalmist pants for God the way a deer pants for flowing streams; his soul thirsts for the living God (Psalm 42:1–2). Jeremiah proclaims God alone as the fountain that gives living water. Any other source, such as the "broken cisterns" (false gods) cannot provide or hold water at all (Jeremiah 2:13).

DISCUSSION QUESTION 2 Living water is the gift of the Holy Spirit, received by faith, that it may flow from the hearts of those who receive it.

DISCUSSION QUESTION 3 God delivers, listens, rescues, provides refuge, and saves. He doesn't let us be put to shame.

DISCUSSION QUESTION 4 Contrasting pairs include the following: falsehood vs. truth; stealing vs. honest work; corrupting talk vs. talk that builds up; bitterness and wrath vs. kindness, tenderheartedness, and forgiveness.

SESSION 5

DAY 1

DISCUSSION QUESTION 1 Jesus was the calm in Martha's storm; He was present in her very home, helping in her time of trouble—in her troubled and anxious state. Jesus, her Refuge, provided rest from her self-inflicted storm of scurry, along with gentle redirection to sit at His feet first.

DISCUSSION QUESTION 2 Wording will vary. Jesus calmed Martha in her self-inflicted storm of scurry, enabling her to find rest in Him: to be still (physically and otherwise), and know that He is God. He gently redirected her to sit first at His feet. He was exalted through her humble service and through her future confession of faith and bold witness that would follow.

DAY 2

DISCUSSION QUESTION 1 Wording will vary, but may include the following: through love and without grumbling, we can show hospitality. We can use our God-given gifts to serve one another by the strength that God supplies, so that He would be glorified through Jesus. We are to serve with our whole heart, as though we are serving the Lord and not other people; it is Christ Himself that we are serving!

DISCUSSION QUESTION 2 Martha expected to serve her guests a meal, along with other services associated with hosting guests in the home. Perhaps that meant providing water, containers, and towels near the door so the guests could wash their feet. She expected Mary to assist with the preparations and the serving. She expected Jesus to tell Mary to help her. Your expectations and answers will be unique to you.

DAY 3

DISCUSSION QUESTION 1 In Luke 13:34, Jesus lamented Jerusalem's eventual destruction and the waywardness of His people, who killed prophets before Him. He longed to gather them all to Himself, but some would reject Him. In Luke 22:31, Jesus tenderly warned Simon Peter of Satan's coming attacks, that Simon Peter would be tested. Again, Jesus is speaking with great affection and concern.

DISCUSSION QUESTION 2 We are to hold fast to the life-giving Word (Philippians 2:16), letting it dwell in us richly so that we grow in both grace and knowledge of our Lord and Savior (2 Peter 3:18).

DISCUSSION QUESTION 3 Answers will vary but may echo Carol's thoughts about the unpopularity of rest, often paralleled with laziness or selfishness; value is given to those who are busy. The impact of busyness may include being swallowed up in stress, feeling that we must constantly strive for something, taking our focus off the Lord, and letting stress sap our energy. Benefits of time with Jesus include, but certainly aren't limited to the following: healing; energizing rest; restoration; peace; clarity; purpose; opportunity to reflect, listen, or simply be; being equipped and prepared.

DAY 4

DISCUSSION QUESTION 1 Love. Without love, we are nothing; we gain nothing; we are only "a noisy gong or a clanging cymbal" (1 Corinthians 13:1).

DISCUSSION QUESTION 2 Your wording will be unique to you, but may include the following: God says to me, "I am with you. I am for you, so who can be against you? I gave up my Son for you; I have given you all that you have. When you cry to Me for help, I hear you; your cry reaches My ears. I am continually with you and hold your hand. You are precious in My eyes and honored; I love you" (see Psalm 18:6; 46:7, 11; 73:23; Isaiah 43:4; Romans 8:31–32).

DAY 5

DISCUSSION QUESTION 1 Names and answers will be unique to you. Someone may effectively speak the truth in love when you share a trusting relationship with them; when past experience proves you can trust their guidance; when they love you, desiring only the best for you.

DISCUSSION QUESTION 2 Martha took Jesus' words to heart. To proclaim her faith as she did (recorded in John 11:27), she certainly spent time at Jesus' feet too.

SESSION 6

DAY 1

DISCUSSION QUESTION 1 Jesus was their safe place to which Martha and Mary could run for shelter and security. He was present with them in His perfect timing (though they didn't think so at first), helping them in grave trouble. Jesus, their Refuge, provided reassurance of His tender love, which was revealed as He wept for and with them in their storm of sadness. He resurrected their brother, and He gave them reassurance of the final resurrection too.

DISCUSSION QUESTION 2 Wording will vary. Jesus came to the sisters at the height of their storm, calming them with His reassurance of the resurrection, and weeping with them. He even calmed their storm in a miraculous way, resurrecting their brother! Even before Jesus raised Lazarus, Martha could be still and know He is God, as she proclaimed Her faith and exalted Him that day. The sisters would continue to give witness to their faith, hosting Jesus in their home and, doubtlessly, spreading the news of His miraculous resurrection of their brother (see John 12:1–8).

DAY 2

DISCUSSION QUESTION 1 By God's love for you, you are called His child (1 John 3:1). In love, Jesus laid down His life (3:16). God's love was made manifest in Jesus—you have life through Him (4:9). He is love, so if you abide in love, you abide in Him (4:16). Because He first loved you, you can love others (4:19).

DISCUSSION QUESTION 2 Martha's great statement of faith preceded Lazarus's miraculous appearance! Her faith was not contingent upon Jesus' immediate action or whether He provided the healing for which she had hoped. In trust, she looked ahead to eternity.

DISCUSSION QUESTION 3 Martha poured out her heart before the Lord Jesus. He was her Refuge in her storm of suffering and deep sadness. She trusted Him "at all times" (Psalm 62:8), even when she knew her brother was dead. She proclaimed salvation in Him. By her faith, she gave Him glory.

DAY 3

DISCUSSION QUESTION 1 Jesus wept over His people's blindness to the truth and the future destruction of Jerusalem (Luke 19:41–42). He wept over His impending death (Hebrews 5:7). And yes, Jesus wept over the death of a dear friend and alongside grieving loved ones (John 11:35).

DISCUSSION QUESTION 2 Answers will vary. The word *our* in Isaiah 53:4 makes this prophesy personal. Jesus bore our burdens and sorrows and carried them for us. Even greater than feeling and knowing our pain, He carried it and bore it for us, in our place.

DISCUSSION QUESTION 3 Jesus engages with Martha in a powerful conversation about faith. Jesus weeps with Mary and asks where Lazarus has been laid. Jesus knew their hearts and what each needed from Him. Jesus' heart is sensitive to our unique needs, and He responds accordingly.

DAY 4

DISCUSSION QUESTION 1 *Imperishable* and *immortality* define the life of victory we have in Christ; we will not perish (that is, die) but have eternal life (see John 3:16). Death no longer has its sting; it has been swallowed up in the victory of life, won for us at Christ's cross. He died for our sin and in our place.

DISCUSSION QUESTION 2 Martha, Mary, and Lazarus hosted a dinner in Jesus' honor, and Mary honored Jesus by anointing His feet with expensive ointment. A large crowd came to see Jesus and Lazarus; as a result, so many people "were going away and believing in Jesus" (John 12:11) that the religious leaders wanted Lazarus killed too. His life proved Jesus' miraculous work. The crowd that saw Jesus raise Lazarus "continued to bear witness" of it (verse 17). The word continued to spread!

DISCUSSION QUESTION 3 Sin brings death: "The wages of sin is death" (Romans 6:23). We are set free "from the law of sin and death" (8:2). God gives the gift of life, by His grace in Christ Jesus, through the Gospel. By faith, the Spirit who "sets you free" (8:2) also "dwells in you" (8:11), enabling you to believe in Christ and receive life. Contrasts from Psalm 30: anger vs. favor; moment vs. lifetime; weeping vs. joy; night vs. morning; mourning vs. dancing and gladness. All point to the sharp contrast between the Law and the Gospel. The Law shows us our sin and our need for a Savior, because sin's wages are death. The Gospel of Christ brings life. God's righteous anger over our sin lasts only a moment in contrast to the overarching favor (God's grace in Christ) that lasts a lifetime. The other contrasts follow, similarly.

DISCUSSION QUESTION 4 Wording will be unique to you but may include the following: eternal life is yours by belief in Jesus Christ, the Son of God (John 6:40). He is the light of the world (1:4). He will raise you up on the Last Day, at His return (6:40). He gives abundant life (10:10). He is life—the only way to the Father (14:6). The Gospel was written so that you may believe and have life in His name (20:31).

DAY 5

DISCUSSION QUESTION 1 We can focus on the things that are seen or on the things that are unseen. We can set our minds on transient and fleeting things or on eternal things. We can find comfort, knowing that our storms and the things of this world are fleeting, not lasting; they will pass, whatever they are. But the things of God are eternal!

DISCUSSION QUESTION 2 Joy; trials; faith; steadfastness; steadfastness; nothing (see James 1:2–4).

DISCUSSION QUESTION 3 You can count on God. He is the light, the guiding star. The wind and sea obey Him. He leads you, marking the path. You can lean upon His strength. He will catch you when you fall. He is with you always. He meets all your needs. He knows what is best. He gives you rest.

SESSION 7

DAY 1

DISCUSSION QUESTION 1 Jesus was Salome's refuge in her storm of self: He was present with her, listening to her, and helping her see the truth in her time of trouble. Jesus gently rebuked her (and her sons), even as He taught the truth, providing crucial reminders of God's plan and the humble ways of His kingdom.

DISCUSSION QUESTION 2 Thanks to Jesus' gentle rebuke and reminders, she could be still; she could stop striving for self-gain. She knew, by Jesus' words, that exaltation in His kingdom meant something so much greater: humble, sacrificial service. She knew that He was God, and she would exalt Him through her continued service, all the way to the tomb at His resurrection.

DAY 2

DISCUSSION QUESTION 1 These women ministered to the traveling group's needs and provided for Jesus and the disciples out of their own means. Their generosity and service said much of their hearts for the Lord and His mission.

DISCUSSION QUESTION 2 Her sons had left the family's livelihood to follow Jesus full-time. If she outlived her husband, she would rely solely on her sons for provision, according to Jewish custom. To see them in places of prominence could benefit her personally.

DISCUSSION QUESTION 3 The context is the Garden of Gethsemane, where Jesus prayed feverishly, just before His arrest. The cup came from the Father; His will was that Christ "drink the cup" of suffering for the sins of the world.

DAY 3

DISCUSSION QUESTION 1 Possible choices include the following: those who "lord it over" or abuse power by exploiting others and dominating, as tyrannical leaders (Matthew 20:25); the stormy circumstances of many nations being the direct results of corrupt leaders misusing their power; people in positions of power for personal or public gain.

DISCUSSION QUESTION 2 Action words or phrases: *despised, rejected, acquainted with grief, esteemed Him not, borne our griefs, carried our sorrows, stricken, smitten, afflicted, pierced, crushed, healed* (we are healed). How He would bear our sins: "pierced for our transgressions" (sins); "with His wounds we are healed" (Isaiah 53:5).

DISCUSSION QUESTION 3 The one-sided adherence to the messianic prophesies was likely so well ingrained into the disciples that they could not consider it to be any other way. More than once, we read that the disciples simply did not understand what Jesus was trying to tell them concerning His imminent death and resurrection. In Luke 18:34, we learn that its meaning was hidden from them.

DISCUSSION QUESTION 4 Answers will vary. Maybe your focus is limited to earthly things when a circumstance, a person, or a temptation vies for your full attention or first priority. Your heart will be where your treasure is, so store up treasures in heaven; they cannot be destroyed or taken from you. Similarly, set your heart and focus on heavenly things—things above! What might help: answers will vary, but may include invaluable time in God's Word with focused attention to the truth; other people of faith who desire the same things because iron sharpens iron; prayer for renewed focus and healthy priorities.

DAY 4

DISCUSSION QUESTION 1 Answers will vary. You were ransomed with the precious blood of Christ.

DISCUSSION QUESTION 2 Answers will vary but may include the following: in our sin, we look to ourselves for satisfaction, but it is fleeting and vain. We are called by God to humbly place others' needs ahead of our own, serving in selfless love, not for selfish gain. It's no wonder we won't find fulfillment in ourselves; that's not how God designed us.

DISCUSSION QUESTION 3 The world may hate you and persecute you (John 15:18–21). You may face a fiery trial, sufferings, and insults (1 Peter 4:13–14). Paul contrasts persecution, "this light momentary affliction" (2 Corinthians 4:17), with future glory with God beyond compare. Some bright spots are that Jesus reminds you that if people keep His Word (listen to Him), they will keep yours too. You can rejoice as you share Christ's sufferings because you will also share in His glory when it is revealed. You are blessed, even when insulted for His name, because the Holy Spirit is upon you!

DISCUSSION QUESTION 4 Jesus washed His disciples' feet, a customary task of the lowest servant of the house. Jesus set an example for His disciples to do for one another what He (their Teacher and Lord) had so humbly done for them.

DAY 5

DISCUSSION QUESTION 1 Worldly greatness stands in stark contrast with greatness in the kingdom of God: great[est] vs. servant; first vs. slave; be served vs. serve; exalts vs. humbled; first vs. last of all and servant of all.

DISCUSSION QUESTION 2 We should keep our eyes on the prize of the call of God in Christ. With our minds on heaven, the place of our citizenship, we await Jesus' return and the final bodily resurrection. We should not set our minds on earthly things or walk as enemies of the cross, whose end is destruction: "they glory in their shame" (Philippians 3:19). As you apply this passage in practical ways, your thoughts and answers will be unique to you.

DISCUSSION QUESTION 3 We can look to our own interests, but not to the extent of selfish ambition. In humility, we count others more significant than ourselves and look to their interests too. In perfect humility, Christ emptied Himself, taking on flesh, becoming a servant for our sakes, obedient to the point of death on a cross (Philippians 2:5–8).

SESSION 8

DAY 1

DISCUSSION QUESTION 1 Jesus was Mary Magdalene's strength in her sorrow and suffering. He was present with her, helping in her time of greatest trouble. Jesus, her Refuge, defeated death by His *resurrection*, providing *restoration* of all believers to the Father and a future *reunion* with all believers in the final *resurrection*.

DISCUSSION QUESTION 2 Jesus stilled the storm that leads to death! As Mary rejoiced in Jesus' resurrection, she could be still and know that He is God. He was her Redeemer who not only restored her to wholeness of health when He cast out demons but also restored her and all believers to a right relationship with God the Father. Jesus was exalted both through His miraculous work in her life and as she proclaimed His resurrection, first immediately to the disciples and then most likely to everyone she met.

DAY 2

This study contains no numbered questions but a series of seven reflections connected to the seven statements of Christ at the cross.

DAY 3

This study (like the last one) contains no numbered questions but several expressions for rest and reflection time in the Word.

DAY 4

DISCUSSION QUESTION 1 Wording will vary but may include the following: "I, the Lord, have redeemed you and called you by name; you are My child. I have engraved you on the palms of My hands, and I love you with an everlasting love. I am continually faithful to you. I know you completely and discern your every thought; I even know when you sit down and when you rise up. I am your heavenly Father" (see Isaiah 43:1; 49:16; Jeremiah 31:3; Psalm 139:1–2; 1 John 3:1).

DISCUSSION QUESTION 2 These events took place after Jesus' resurrection too. In Luke 24, Jesus joined two disciples on the road to Emmaus, but they were kept from recognizing Him until He broke bread and blessed it; then He immediately vanished from their sight. In John 21, Jesus called from shore as the disciples fished from their boat, but they did not know it was Him until they followed His instructions for a miraculous catch of fish.

DAY 5

DISCUSSION QUESTION 1 God knows our hearts, our needs, and our prayers. He miraculously works through our prayers and those of others, orchestrating countless things together for good. We grow in faith through prayer.

DISCUSSION QUESTION 2 In our hearts and minds we make plans, but the Lord establishes our steps (Proverbs 16:9). His purpose will stand (Proverbs 19:21). He is necessarily with us, since He is establishing the steps we take. He is giving us strength for every step, working His purpose through the fruition of those plans, according to His will. The words of these proverbs provide comfort, because we know we are not alone in the orchestration of any plan. He leads our steps, and He will use our plans for His purpose.

SOURCES

Quotations from Gary P. Baumler, *John*, People's Bible Commentary, copyright © 2005 Concordia Publishing House. All rights reserved.

Quotations from Deb Burma, *Stepping Out: To a Life on the Edge*, copyright © 2013 Deb Burma, published by Concordia Publishing House. All rights reserved.

Quotations from Edward A. Engelbrecht, ed., *Concordia's Complete Bible Handbook*, second edition, copyright © 2013 Concordia Publishing House. All rights reserved.

Quotations from Edward A. Engelbrecht, ed., *Lutheran Bible Companion*, volume 2, copyright © 2014 Concordia Publishing House. All rights reserved.

Quotations from Michael Eschelbach, *The Big Book of New Testament Questions and Answers*, copyright © 2015 Michael Eschelbach, published by Concordia Publishing House. All rights reserved.

Quotations from Sharla Fritz, *Waiting: A Bible Study on Patience, Hope, and Trust*, copyright © 2017 Sharla Fritz, published by Concordia Publishing House. All rights reserved.

Quotations from Jane Fryar, ed., *Today's Light Devotional Bible*, copyright © 2014 Concordia Publishing House. All rights reserved.

Quotations from Michael W. Newman, *Hope When Your Heart Breaks: Navigating Grief and Loss*, copyright © 2017 Michael W. Newman, published by Concordia Publishing House. All rights reserved.

Quotations from Daniel E. Paavola, *Mark*, Reformation Heritage Bible Commentary, copyright © 2013 Concordia Publishing House. All rights reserved.

Quotations from Victor H. Prange, *Luke*, People's Bible Commentary, copyright © 2004 Concordia Publishing House. All rights reserved.

Quotations from Walter R. Roehrs and Martin H. Franzmann, *Concordia Self-Study Commentary*, copyright © 1979 Concordia Publishing House. All rights reserved.

Quotations from Timothy Saleska, *Psalms 1–50*, Concordia Commentary, copyright © 2020 Concordia Publishing House. All rights reserved.

Quotations from Robert A. Sorensen, *Luke*, Reformation Heritage Bible Commentary, copyright © 2014 Concordia Publishing House. All rights reserved.

Quotations from David R. Steele and Diane L. Bahn, *Jesus: A Study on the Words of Matthew, Mark, Luke, and John*, copyright © 2020 David R. Steele and Diane L. Bahn, published by Concordia Publishing House. All rights reserved.

Quotations from Marlys Taege Moberg, *The Heart of Jesus: Women in the Gospel of Luke*, copyright © 2009 Marlys Taege Moberg, published by Concordia Publishing House. All rights reserved.

Quotations from Tim Wesemann, *Seasons under the Son: Stories of Grace*, copyright © 2002 Tim Wesemann, published by Concordia Publishing House. All rights reserved.

Quotations from *Portals of Prayer* copyright © 2019 Concordia Publishing House. All rights reserved.

ENDNOTES

1   Edward A. Engelbrecht, ed., *The Lutheran Study Bible (TLSB)* (St. Louis: Concordia Publishing House, 2009), 891.

2   Timothy E. Saleska, *Psalms 1–50*, Concordia Commentary (St. Louis: Concordia Publishing House, 2020), 701.

3   Saleska, 698–99.

4   Robert G. Hoerber, ed., *Concordia Self-Study Bible* (St. Louis: Concordia Publishing House, 1986), 832.

5   Walter H. Roehrs and Martin H. Franzmann, *Concordia Self-Study Commentary* (St. Louis: Concordia Publishing House, 1979), Psalms, 363.

6   John Parsons, "Torah of Surrender . . . God's Irrepressible Care of the World," Hebrew for Christians, https://www.hebrew4christians.com/Meditations/Be_Still/be_still.html (accessed November 3, 2020).

7   Hoerber, 833.

8   Saleska, 700.

9   Roehrs and Franzmann, Psalms, 363.

10   Edward A. Engelbrecht, ed., *Concordia's Complete Bible Handbook*, second edition (St. Louis: Concordia Publishing House, 2013), 166–67.

11   Fryar, 1656.

12   Debbie Larson, "Separation—but Not from God!" Lutheran Women in Mission, http://blog.lwml.org/2020/03/separation-but-not-from-god (accessed November 3, 2020); used by permission.

13   Courtney Limmer, Instagram post, April 27, 2020; used by permission.

14   Karen Sue Murdy, "Courage through the Covid-19 Storm," *Rejoice in the Lord Always . . . Joy in the Journey!* https://karensuemurdy.blogspot.com/2020 (accessed November 3, 2020); used by permission.

15   Carol Fedewa, Facebook post, March 26, 2020, https://www.facebook.com/groups/hclcwomensministry/permalink/3166929616665185 (accessed December 10, 2020); used by permission.

16   Katie Anderson, e-mail to author, May 12, 2020; used by permission.

17   Katie Anderson, text to author, June 25, 2020; used by permission.

18   Baumler, Gary P., *John*, People's Bible Commentary (St. Louis: Concordia Publishing House, 2005), 122.

19   *TLSB*, 1796.

20   Baumler, 122.

21	Church of the Great God, "Greek/Hebrew Definitions: Grapho," Bible Tools, https://www.bibletools.org/index.cfm/fuseaction/Lexicon.show/ID/G1125/grapho.htm (accessed November 5, 2020).

22	*TLSB*, 1796.

23	Michael W. Newman, *Hope When Your Heart Breaks: Navigating Grief and Loss* (St. Louis: Concordia Publishing House, 2017), 99.

24	Hoerber, 1622.

25	*TLSB*, 1796.

26	Online Parallel Bible Project, "Strong's Greek: 1135," Bible Hub, https://biblehub.com/greek/1135.htm (accessed November 5, 2020).

27	Connie Johnson, conversations with the author, April–June 2020; used by permission.

28	Deb Burma, *Stepping Out: To a Life on the Edge* (St. Louis: Concordia Publishing House, 2013), 80–82.

29	Online Parallel Bible Project, "Strong's Greek: 131," Bible Hub, https://biblehub.com/greek/131.htm. (accessed November 5, 2020).

30	Mayo Clinic Staff, "Menorrhagia (Heavy Menstrual Bleeding)," Mayo Clinic, https://www.mayoclinic.org/diseases-conditions/menorrhagia/symptoms-causes/syc-20352829 (accessed November 5, 2020).

31	Engelbrecht, *Handbook*, 314.

32	Daniel E. Paavola, *Mark*, Reformation Heritage Bible Commentary (St. Louis: Concordia Publishing House, 2013), 92.

33	F. W. Farrar, *Cambridge Bible for Schools and Colleges* (Cambridge: Cambridge University Press, 1891), as quoted by Online Parallel Bible Project, "Luke 8:43 Commentaries," Biblehub, https://biblehub.com/commentaries/luke/8-43.htm (accessed November 24, 2020).

34	Marlys Taege Moberg, *The Heart of Jesus: Women in the Gospel of Luke* (St. Louis: Concordia Publishing House, 2009), 121.

35	Paavola, 92.

36	Victor H. Prange, *Luke*, People's Bible Commentary (St. Louis: Concordia Publishing House, 2004), 100.

37	Paavola, 93.

38	Hoerber, 1564.

39	Robert A. Sorensen, *Luke*, Reformation Heritage Bible Commentary (St. Louis: Concordia Publishing House, 2014), 156.

40	Fryar, 1372.

41	Taege Moberg, 123.

42	Hoerber, 1564.

43	Mayo Clinic Staff, "Anxiety Disorders," Mayo Clinic, https://www.mayoclinic.org/diseases-conditions/anxiety/symptoms-causes/syc-20350961 (accessed November 5, 2020).

44	"Is Mental Illness Physical or Mental?" Mental Health America, https://screening.mhanational.org/content/mental-illness-physical-or-mental (accessed November 5, 2020).

45   Newman, 107.

46   Newman, 95–96.

47   Based on Courtney Limmer, video Facebook post, May 7, 2020, https://www.facebook .com/OurFatherLutheran/videos/623530894907537 (accessed December 10, 2020); used by permission.

48   Karen Sue Murdy, "Courage through the Covid-19 Storm: Do Not Worry about Tomorrow," *Rejoice in the Lord Always . . . Joy in the Journey!* https://karensuemurdy.blogspot.com/2020/04 /courage-through-covid-19-storm-do-not.html (accessed November 5, 2020); used by permission.

49   Hoerber, 1511.

50   Burma, 38.

51   Engelbrecht, *Handbook*, 345.

52   Engelbrecht, *Handbook*, 344.

53   Baumler, 61.

54   Engelbrecht, *Handbook*, 345.

55   Hoerber, 1610.

56   Brené Brown, "Listening to Shame," TED: Ideas Worth Spreading, March 2012, 17:42, https:// www.ted.com/talks/brene_brown_listening_to_shame (accessed November 6, 2020); used by permission.

57   Stacey Holt, conversations with the author, May 2019; used by permission.

58   David R. Steele and Diane L. Bahn, *Jesus: A Study on the Words of Matthew, Mark, Luke, and John* (St. Louis: Concordia Publishing House, 2020), 53, 56.

59   Burma, 47.

60   Hoerber, 1610.

61   *TLSB*, 1787.

62   Baumler, 67.

63   Walter R. Roehrs and Martin H. Franzmann, *Concordia Self-Study Commentary* (St. Louis: Concordia Publishing House, 1979), John, 90.

64   Carol Fedewa, Facebook post, March 24, 2020, https://www.facebook.com/groups /hclcwomensministry/permalink/3162239357134211 (accessed December 10, 2020); used by permission.

65   Newman, 98.

66   Dina Spector, "Here's How Many Days a Person Can Survive without Water," *Business Insider*, https://www.businessinsider.com/how-many-days-can-you-survive-without-water-2014-5 (accessed November 5, 2020).

67   Saleska, 702.

68   Saleska, 701.

69   Anonymous friend of the author, e-mail to author; used by permission.

70   *TLSB*, 1735.

71   Taege Moberg, 136.

72   Church of the Great God, "Greek/Hebrew Definitions: merimnao," Bible Tools, https:// www.bibletools.org/index.cfm/fuseaction/Lexicon.show/ID/G3309/merimnao.htm (accessed November 9, 2020).

73   Online Parallel Bible Project, "Strong' Greek: 2350," Bible Hub, https://biblehub.com/str /greek/2350.htm (accessed November 19, 2020).

74   Church of the Great God, "Greek/Hebrew Definitions: perispao," Bible Tools, https:// www.bibletools.org/index.cfm/fuseaction/Lexicon.show/ID/G4049/perispao.htm (accessed November 9, 2020).

75   Taege Moberg, 150.

76   Elizabeth Bruick, e-mail to author, May 2020; used by permission.

77   Sorensen, 255.

78   Prange, 127.

79   Carol Fedewa, Facebook post, February 5, 2020, https://www.facebook.com/groups /hclcwomensministry/permalink/3045138848844263 (accessed December 10, 2020); used by permission.

80   Sorensen, 204.

81   Sorensen, 144.

82   Taege Moberg, 143.

83   Sorensen, 205.

84   Jonathon Krenz, "The Good Portion," *Portals of Prayer* vol. 82, no. 444 (2019), July 21.

85   Elizabeth Bruick, e-mail to author, May 2020; used by permission.

86   Michelle Diercks, "How Can We Be Still in Circumstances beyond Our Control?" *Peace in His Presence*, podcast, https://podcasts.apple.com/us/podcast/how-can-we-be-still-in -circumstances-beyond-our-control/id1443248237?i=1000469908308 (accessed December 10, 2020); used by permission.

87   Diercks, *Peace in His Presence*; used by permission.

88   Sidewalk Prophet, e-mail newsletter; used by permission.

89   Sidewalk Prophets, e-mail newsletter; used by permission.

90   Baumler, 159.

91   Baumler, 160.

92   Roehrs and Franzmann, John, 95.

93   *TLSB*, 1803.

94   Sharla Fritz, *Waiting: A Bible Study on Patience, Hope, and Trust* (St. Louis: Concordia Publishing House, 2017), 119.

95   Fritz, 119.

96   *TLSB*, 1803.

97   *TLSB*, 1804.

98   Edward A. Engelbrecht, ed., *Lutheran Bible Companion*, vol. 2 (St. Louis: Concordia Publishing House, 2014), 335–36.

99   Newman, 20.

100   Steele and Bahn, 134.

101   Fryar, 1465.

102   See Church of the Great God, "Greek/Hebrew Definitions: doxa," Bible Tools, https://www
.bibletools.org/index.cfm/fuseaction/Lexicon.show/ID/G1391/doxa.htm (accessed November
9, 2020).

103   See Church of the Great God, "Greek/Hebrew Definitions: doxazo," Bible Tools, https://
www.bibletools.org/index.cfm/fuseaction/Lexicon.show/ID/G1392/doxazo.htm   (accessed
November 9, 2020).

104   Roehrs and Franzmann, John, 95.

105   Newman, 64.

106   Molly Dixon, messages to author, July 3, 2020; used by permission.

107   Wendysue Fluegge, "Be Still," audio recording, 1996, https://www.wendysue.com (accessed
November 10, 2020), reprinted with permission.

108   Myra Case, e-mail to author, April 1, 2020; used by permission.

109   Myra Case, e-mail to author, April 1, 2020; used by permission.

110   Paavola, 191.

111   Hoerber, 1478.

112   Burma, 140.

113   *TLSB*, 1626.

114   *TLSB*, 1808.

115   Walter R. Roehrs and Martin H. Franzmann, *Concordia Self-Study Commentary* (St. Louis:
Concordia Publishing House, 1979), Mark, 51.

116   Paavola, 193.

117   Sarah Schultz, Facebook post, April 13, 2020; used by permission.

118   Tim Wesemann, *Seasons under the Son: Stories of Grace* (St. Louis: Concordia Publishing House,
2002), 119.

119   Sorensen, 144.

120   *TLSB*, 1725.

121   Steele and Bahn, 172.

122   Taege Moberg, 190–91.

123   Dictionary.com, "excruciating," https://www.dictionary.com/browse/excruciating (accessed
November 10, 2020).

124   Taege Moberg, 190.

125   Steele and Bahn, 174.

126   Sorensen, 403.

127   Based on Karen Lippert, "Soul Amnesia," Women's Leadership Institute, http://wlicuw.org
/soul-amnesia-3 (accessed November 10, 2020); used by permission.

128   See Online Parallel Bible Project, "Strong's Greek: 2799," Bible Hub, https://biblehub.com
/greek/2799.htm (accessed November 10, 2020).

129   Steele and Bahn, 177.

130   Michael Eschelbach, *The Big Book of New Testament Questions and Answers* (St. Louis: Concordia Publishing House, 2015), 294.

131   *TLSB*, 1825.

132   Baumler, 260.

133   Steele and Bahn, 177.

134   Baumler, 261.

ACKNOWLEDGMENTS

Be Still and Know began long ago. As I heard the stormy circumstances of women around me, and as I struggled through storms of my own, I kept coming back to God's soothing words in Psalm 46. *Be Still and Know* began as a women's retreat. When women heard the theme, so many said it appeared to be written just for them because they needed to hear these words. Thank you, sisters in Christ who have been on retreat with me, so we may be still together. You listened and learned, shared and encouraged; you held one another up in your own personal storms.

A huge shout-out goes to my family: my husband, Cory, who was faithful to provide a box of exquisite chocolates to cheer me toward the finish line. I savored one (or two) per day as I wrapped up my writing time. Love you more! My kids, who have prayed for me and encouraged me from near and far—I cannot **thank you** enough!

More than forty friends and loved ones have contributed to this study, sharing storm stories, quotes, or life with me. **Thank you** for adding so much to this work and to my life, and for allowing me to use your stories or share your hearts. Still others joined me for coffee, prayed with me, or held my hand in some way, whether face-to-face or from far away. **Thank you!**

I cannot say enough about my CPH team: Peggy, Elizabeth, Laura, Holli, Lindsey, Cheryl, Alex, Joe, Anna, and others! **Thank you** for your support and encouragement, editing expertise, marketing marvels, stellar graphic design skills, video production, and more. You are the best!

I have shed tears while sitting in awe, time and again, over God's plan and timing, that I would wrap up this Bible study during a pandemic storm and at a time of so much unrest in our nation. I believe this theme carries with it, more powerfully than ever (were that possible), a message we desperately need to hear amid every storm. God alone is our refuge, our strength, and our ever-present help in trouble. We can be still amid any storm because we know this truth: He is God. He is all-powerful to save and to protect, to provide strength and help. He is exalted above all. So, above all, I THANK YOU, Lord Jesus, my refuge and my strength!

Be still,

Deb

NOTES

NOTES